INSIGHTS
2020

Junko Murao
Akiko Miyama
Atsushi Mukuhira
Tomoko Tsujimoto
Ashley Moore

KINSEIDO

Kinseido Publishing Co., Ltd.

3-21 Kanda Jimbo-cho, Chiyoda-ku,
Tokyo 101-0051, Japan

First published 2020 by Kinseido Publishing Co., Ltd.

　このテキストは、文化・環境・技術・経済・社会・教育・医療・観光・農業といった幅広い分野の記事を取り上げています。今や世界はさらにグローバル化され、地球人という意識を持って生きる時代にあるように思われます。生きた英語を学びながら、そのような現状に応じたより広い視野を養えるよう国内外の様々なトピックの記事を選んでおります。これらのトピックは、ディスカッションの話題としても活用できるでしょう。本テキストを授業内での様々な活動にお役立て頂ければと思います。

●**Key Expressions 1**
　写真などの視覚情報を見てトピックへの関心を促す、リーディング・セクション読解のためのキーワードのブランク埋めの問題です。キーワードを耳で聞くだけでなく、最初の一文字と語数をヒントにして、辞書も参照しながら解答してみてください。リーディング・セクションの背景知識を構築しながら、辞書を用いて文法も確認する練習問題となっています。

●**Key Expressions 2**
　リーディング・セクション中に登場する重要表現や、TOEIC にも出現頻度の高い語彙を学習するエクササイズです。単なるキーワードの意味理解だけでなく、関連語句や派生語を構成する接頭辞・接尾辞の意味など、単語力増強に必要な情報が盛り込まれています。

●**Key Expressions 3**
　話題に関連した構文や語法の練習問題です。基礎的な文法力も試せる問題となっています。

●**Background Knowledge**
　リーディング・セクションの背景を構築する短い記事を読み、簡単な速読用の設問を解きます。一語一句訳すのではなく、必要な情報のみを拾い読みするという速読方法（スキャニング）で読んでみて下さい。語彙の類推力を養うために、問題解答に関係するところには、あえて注は付けておりませんので、辞書を参照せずに解答してみましょう。

●**Newspaper English**
　文法確認のセクションです。ただし、網羅的に文法を扱ってはいません。英文記事を読むために最低限必要な文法の基礎知識や表現ルールを学びます。

●**Reading**
　本セクションを読むまでに、かなりの背景知識・文法・語彙の構築ができています。ここまでのセクションをしっかり復習しておけば、辞書なしでもほぼ理解できるでしょう。読解の助けになる注は付けていますが、できるだけ注を参照しないで読むよう心がけてください。

●**Summary, Comprehension 1&2**
　リーディング・セクションの内容が理解できているかどうかのチェックを行います。

　以上のようなヴァラエティに富んだ練習問題によって、英字新聞やインターネットのニュース記事を抵抗感なく読めるようになるはずです。最後になりましたが、テキスト作成の際にお世話になりました金星堂編集部の皆様に心からお礼を申し上げます。

編著者

　英字新聞を目の前にすると、一体どこからどのように読んでいけばよいのか迷う人もいるでしょう。まずは、以下のジャパンタイムズ紙のフロントページ（第一面）やジャパンニューズ紙のオンライン版トップページを見ながら、英字新聞を読む際に知っておくべきことを学びましょう。大きなニュースは繰り返しフロントページで取り上げられることがあります。まずはこのページで、持続性があり、興味を持てる話題を選択し、しばらくそのニュースを追いかけていく読み方がお勧めです。同じ話題のニュースに何度も触れていると、次第に辞書なしで読めるようになるでしょう。

1. 紙媒体のフロントページの構成

新聞社のロゴ（Logo）

これは紙媒体のジャパンタイムズ紙のフロントページです。ジャパンタイムズ紙は、ニューヨークタイムズ紙とセットで発行されており、国内・海外の情報を幅広く提供しています。

重要記事の紹介

各紙面から大きなニュースを取り上げ簡単に説明しています。

ヘッドライン（Headline）

→ヘッドラインの詳しい説明は p.6 参照。

リード（Lead）

記事の書き出しの一段落目のことをリードと呼びます。ニュースの概略が紹介されます。リードには、5W1Hの情報ができるだけ盛り込まれます。

キャプション（Caption）

図版や写真につく説明文のことです。記事を読むときの大切な背景知識を提供しています。先に目を通しておくと記事の理解の助けとなります。

目次

記事のジャンルと掲載ページが提示されています。

２．オンライン版のトップページ

新聞社のロゴ（Logo）

これは読売新聞の英語版ジャパンニューズ紙のトップページです。紙媒体とは異なり、文字数を減らし、視覚情報の多い作りとなっています。

記事のカテゴリー

各項目をクリックすると、政治・社会・ビジネス・スポーツなどのカテゴリー別の記事を、日をさかのぼって読むことができます。

トップニュース
（Top News）

紙媒体のフロントページに載る重要記事が紹介されます。ヘッドラインをクリックすると記事全体が読めます。

各種特集ページへのリンク

書評や日本文化紹介など、旬な話題が集められています。

その他の重要記事や特集の紹介

3. ヘッドラインの特徴 ─────────────

　ヘッドラインの英文はいくつかのルールに則って書かれています。文字数を少なくし、簡潔に表現するための工夫がなされます。以下にもっともよく使用されるルールをあげますので参考にしてください。

① 記事を新鮮に見せる「現在形」
過去・現在完了の内容であっても、記事を新鮮に見せるために動詞を現在形にすることがよくあります。
China stocks fall sharply「中国株価急落」

② 進行形・受動態における be 動詞の省略
「進行形・近接未来」や「受動態」では be 動詞が省略され、それぞれ、V-ing や V-ed の形で表されます。
America struggling to fight mosquito-borne diseases「アメリカ、蚊が媒介する病と格闘」
Narita website hit by cyberattacks「成田空港ウェブサイト、サイバー攻撃に遭う」

③ 未来を表す不定詞（to V）
Russia to cut space program budget「ロシア宇宙計画予算を削減予定」

④ 冠詞・be 動詞の省略
Caregivers in short supply in aging Japan「高齢化の日本、介護者不足」

⑤ say(s) の代わりに用いるコロン(:)
Deforestation threatens pygmies: study「森林破壊がピグミーの生存を脅かしていると、ある調査」

⑥ 省略や略語の多用
Govt ← Government（政府）　　BOJ ← The Bank of Japan（日本銀行）　　HK ← Hong Kong（香港）
VW ← Volkswagen（フォルクスワーゲン）　　uni prof. ← university professor（大学教授）

⑦ カンマによる and の省略
Japan, US, South Korea diplomats to meet in Tokyo「日本、アメリカ、韓国外交官、東京で会合」

⑧ 好んで使われる短い綴りの語
eye「目をつける」　　OK「承認する」　　vie「競う」　　ink「署名する」

4. 英字新聞攻略法 ─────────────

　さて、新聞全体の構成がわかったところで、どのように英字新聞に親しんでいけばいいのでしょうか。以下に、英字新聞に慣れるためのコツを紹介します。

① 英字新聞の言語的特徴に慣れよう
英字新聞では、ニュースを新鮮に見せるために **3. ヘッドラインの特徴** で見たように、ヘッドラインを現在形で書くなど、読者を引きつける様々な工夫がなされています。本書では、それらの工夫に関して **Newspaper English** のセクションで取り上げていますので、問題に解答しながら、その特徴を覚えましょう。

② すべての記事を読む必要はない
すべての記事を隅々まで読むのは大変ですし、その必要もありません。まずは、ヘッドラインや写真などを見て、興味のある記事だけを読んでみましょう。英字新聞に慣れるまでは、できるだけ日本に関する記事を選ぶほうが読みやすいでしょう。

③ リード・写真・キャプションは、最初に目を通そう
リード、写真、キャプションは背景知識を提供する役目を果たしています。記事の本文は、リードに最重要情報が置かれ、パラグラフが進むにつれ情報の重要度が下がっていきますから、しばらくはリードだけに挑戦するのもよいでしょう。

④ 特定のテーマに絞って読むようにしよう
特定のテーマを継続して読む方法が英語学習には最適です。あるテーマに特有の語彙をまとめて学習することができるので、次第に類似テーマの記事なら簡単に読めるようになっていきます。

Insights 2020　Table of Contents

Chapter 1

Books! Bringing a Bright Future to Children
子どもたちの未来のための図書館

Miyu Ozawa

● **Key Expressions 1**　　　　　　　　　　　　⊙ CD1-02

写真に関する音声を聞いて1〜3の（　　）内に適当な語を書き入れましょう。

1. Miyu Ozawa is (s _ _ _ _ _ _ _ _ _) by primary schoolchildren in Cambodia.
   小澤未侑さん（写真中央）が、カンボジアで小学生たちに囲まれている。

2. Instead of spending the gift money, she thought that she would use it for useful (p _ _ _ _ _ _ _).
   彼女は、貰ったお金を使わずに、それを有益な目的のために使おうと考えた。

3. She decided to use her (s _ _ _ _ _ _) and make a library where children could study on their own.
   彼女は貯金を使って、子どもたちが一人で勉強できる図書館を作ることを決意した。

● **Key Expressions 2**

以下の1～7は科目の名称です。日本語に対応する科目名を選択肢から選び、（　　　）内
に書き入れましょう。

1. 算数　　　　　（　　　　　　　　　　　　　　　　　　）
2. 体育　　　　　（　　　　　　　　　　　　　　　　　　）
3. 道徳　　　　　（　　　　　　　　　　　　　　　　　　）
4. 理科　　　　　（　　　　　　　　　　　　　　　　　　）
5. 社会　　　　　（　　　　　　　　　　　　　　　　　　）
6. 図画工作　　　（　　　　　　　　　　　　　　　　　　）
7. 数学　　　　　（　　　　　　　　　　　　　　　　　　）

> ethics　　　arithmetic　　　science　　　social studies
> mathematics　　　physical education　　　arts and crafts

● **Key Expressions 3**

以下の1～3の英文の（　　　）内の動詞を適当な形にしましょう。

1. Akiko Suzuki of the Shanti Volunteer Association said, "I want to encourage
   her by (continue →　　　　　　　　　) to do what little we can. I believe
   that the power of books will allow people (live →　　　　　　　　) better
   lives."
   公益社団法人シャンティ国際ボランティア会の鈴木晶子さんは、「微力ながら私た
   ちができる限りのことをし続けることで彼女を励ましたいです。本の力によって、
   人々がより良い暮らしができるようになると信じています」と話した。

2. After (return →　　　　　　　　　) to Japan, Ozawa began thinking about
   (build →　　　　　　　　) a library in Cambodia.
   日本に戻ってから、小澤さんはカンボジアに図書館を建てることを考え始めた。

3. "I hope some will aspire (be →　　　　　　　　) teachers after encountering
   books," Ozawa said.
   「私は、本に出会ったら先生になりたいと思う人たちが出てくると思います」と小
   澤さんは語った。

カンボジアの小学校の現状について、英文に<u>述べられていないもの</u>を1～4から選びましょう。

In Cambodia, schools were destroyed and textbooks were burned during the 1975-1979 reign of Khmer Rouge leader Pol Pot. It is believed that some 1.7 million people died from torture, massacre, hunger and other causes.

To this day, the country is still short of teachers. Ensuring the quality of instructors is another lingering problem.

Ozawa chose a primary school in the village of Cham as a candidate site. The village is in Prey Veng province, a rural area close to the border with Vietnam. The school has 30-odd pupils and only one teacher.

The Asahi Shimbun

Notes Khmer Rouge「クメール・ルージュ（かつてのカンボジアの政治勢力で、武装勢力）」　torture「拷問」　massacre「虐殺」　lingering「長引く」

1. カンボジアの学校はクメール・ルージュの指導者ポル・ポト政権時に破壊された。

2. 現在も教員不足と教育の質が問題となっている。

3. 小澤さんはチャム村の小学校を候補地として選んだ。

4. その学校のあるプレイベン州には30世帯が暮らしている。

● **Newspaper English**

 共起表現（コロケーション）とは、よく使用される語と語の組み合わせのことです。この組み合わせをたくさん知っていると新聞英語も読みやすくなります。

次の英文の1と2の（　　）内の語のうち適当な語を選び、文章を完成させましょう。

1. Her mother used to tell her not to spend the money on games or for (having / making) fun.
彼女の母親は、そのお金をゲームや娯楽に使わないようにと言っていた。

2. (Spanking / Flashing) new desks and chairs were also purchased.
新品の机と椅子も購入された。

Japanese teen funds library for Cambodian school out of her own pocket

OSAKA — Instead of spending the gift money she received each New Year and on entering school, Miyu Ozawa saved it for her future. Thanks to her savings, primary schoolchildren in Cambodia are on a path to a brighter future.

These children are the beneficiaries of a new library 5 funded by Ozawa, 16, a second-year student at Tezukayama Gakuin Senior High School in Osaka.

"I had saved the money, which my mother used to tell me not to spend on games or for having fun," she said. "That turned out to be useful in the end." 10

During her spring vacation following her graduation from junior high school, Ozawa worked as a volunteer on a 10-day tour in Cambodia, where she helped with classes at a primary school.

While skipping rope with the children, Ozawa turned to 15 one girl and asked her in English, with gestures, what she felt happiest doing. The girl looked Ozawa squarely in the eye and said, "Studying."

After returning to Japan, Ozawa began thinking about building a library in Cambodia because it appeared that 20 while the country had schools, it did not have enough teachers or teaching materials.

"Books will give them the first step for studying on their own," Ozawa said. "I hope some will aspire to be teachers after encountering books." 25

Ozawa recalled a male teacher as saying, "The classes here are centered on arithmetic because life would be difficult without a minimum knowledge of math. I had never even thought of a library before. I would really like to have one here." 30

A room in the school building was repainted and furnished with 30 copies each of an English textbook and a schoolbook

beneficiary 「受益者」

used to... 「かつて~だった」

squarely 「まっすぐに、まともに」

furnish ~ with... 「~に…を備え付ける」

for the local Khmer script. Spanking new desks and chairs were also purchased.

The total cost of $6,000 (670,000 yen) was funded by Ozawa's savings.

5 Ozawa visited the primary school for the first time this past summer, where she found herself in the company of smiling children. The name "Miyu's Educational Library" was later engraved on an outer wall.

The Asahi Shimbun

Khmer script 「クメール文字」

in the company of... 「〜と一緒にいて、〜に囲まれて」
engrave... 「〜を刻む」

● **Summary** CD1-05

以下の空所 1 〜 4 に当てはまる語を選択肢から選び、書き入れましょう。

A Japanese (1.   ), Miyu Ozawa, has used her savings to fund a library for primary schoolchildren in Cambodia. She first went to the (2.   ) as part of a 10-day volunteer tour. During the tour, she was struck by both the (3.   ) of the children for learning and the (4.   ) of teachers and teaching materials. Her money, which she saved for a long time, has helped to pay for books and furniture and redecorate the new library.

| country | lack | passion | schoolgirl |

● Comprehension 1

以下の 1 〜 4 の英文について、小澤さんの行ったこととして本文の内容に合っているものには T（True）を、合っていないものには F（False）を（　　）内に書き入れましょう。

1. She worked as a volunteer in Cambodia for a month. （　　）
2. While teaching arithmetic, she asked one of the schoolchildren what she felt happiest doing. （　　）
3. She used to save her pocket money for having fun. （　　）
4. Her money paid for 60 books and some chairs and desks. （　　）

● Comprehension 2

本文の内容に合うように、1 の質問の答えとして適当なものを、2 と 3 の英文を完成させるのに適当なものを a 〜 d から選びましょう。

1. Which of the following statements about Miyu Ozawa's mother is true?
   a. She was very surprised by her daughter's unusual decision.
   b. She insisted that Miyu donate her savings to schools in Cambodia.
   c. She has worked for many years as a librarian in Osaka.
   d. She had certain ideas about how her daughter should use her savings.

2. On returning to Japan, Ozawa recalled that Cambodia had a shortage of
   a. educational materials.
   b. school buildings.
   c. Japanese textbooks.
   d. sports equipment.

3. Since the library was built,
   a. the Japanese government has equaled Ozawa's contribution.
   b. poems have been written on the walls in Khmer.
   c. it has been named after its young benefactor.
   d. Ozawa has moved to Cambodia to train as a teacher.

Chapter 2

Brew Sake with Fresh Ideas!

伝統への新たなる挑戦

Kyodo News

● Key Expressions 1

CD1-06

写真に関する音声を聞いて1〜3の（　　　）内に適当な語を書き入れましょう。

1. Two foreign (n _ _ _ _ _ _ _ _) are working as apprentices in one of Japan's most traditional industries.

2人の外国人が日本の最も伝統的な産業の一つにおいて、見習い生として働いている。

2. They not only discovered the intricacies of sake, but they also came to understand the unique (a _ _ _ _ _ _) of working in the sake brewery.

2人は酒の奥深さを発見しただけでなく、酒の醸造所で働く独特の側面も理解するようになった。

3. Nishiyama Shuzojo Co. has tried to (m _ _ _ _ _ _ _ _) its company practices, including hiring women and foreign nationals at its *kura* (brewery) from around 2013.

株式会社西山酒造場は、2013年頃から蔵（醸造所）で女性や外国人を雇用するなど、会社の慣習を近代化するよう努めてきた。

● Key Expressions 2

形容詞に -ness や -cy といった接尾辞をつけて名詞を形成するものがあります。
-ness は「性質・程度・状態」、-cy は「性質・状態・作用」といった意味を持ちます。

以下の 1 〜 5 の形容詞に枠内のいずれかの接尾辞をつけて名詞を作りましょう。

1. intricate（複雑な）　　　　　　　　　[　　　　　　　　　]（奥深さ）
2. attentive（注意深い、思いやりのある）　[　　　　　　　　　]（気遣い、気配り）
3. accurate（正確な）　　　　　　　　　[　　　　　　　　　]（正確さ）
4. unique（唯一の、独特の）　　　　　　[　　　　　　　　　]（独自性）
5. fluent（流暢な）　　　　　　　　　　[　　　　　　　　　]（流暢さ）

● Key Expressions 3

以下の 1 〜 4 の英文の（　）内に当てはまる語を選択肢から選び、書き入れましょう。

1. Kaminsky and Chen take part in almost (　　　　　　　　) step of the brewing process.

   カミンスキーさんとチェンさんは酒の醸造過程のほとんどすべての段階に加わっている。

2. "I think some people would leave the company for this in Taiwan. I thought 'doing calisthenics exercises has (　　　　　　　　) to do with the work', but I got used to it," said a laughing Chen.

   「台湾ではこのために会社を辞める人もいると思います。柔軟体操をすることは仕事には全く関係がないと思いましたが、慣れました」とチェンさんは笑いながら話した。

3. "I'm still not sure if I (　　　　　　　　) understand Japanese culture," Kaminsky said.

   「日本文化を完全に理解しているかどうかまだ分かりません」とカミンスキーさんは述べた。

4. "You could make the same sake, but each time there's going to be (　　　　　　　　) that's a little bit different, so that's always interesting," Kaminsky said.

   「同じ酒を造ることはできるかもしれませんが、毎回少しだけ違うところが出てきます。だからいつも面白いんです」とカミンスキーさんは話した。

| something | nothing | every | fully |

西山酒造場について、英文に述べられているものを1〜4から選びましょう。

Reflecting Nishiyama Shuzojo's motto — "Good products are made in a good atmosphere" — the company encourages its workplace to be joyful.

The employees' cheery voices, combined with the rich aroma generated by the fermentation process, seem to bring happiness to visitors even before they get a taste of the product, which is now exported to 24 countries. The company has also developed other products such as yogurts and cakes, using sake-brewing techniques.

Kyodo

1. 西山酒造場では、職場を楽しい場にしようとがんばっている。
2. この会社では酒の発酵過程を促進するため元気な声であいさつをすることにしている。
3. 24か国以上の人々が今までこの会社を訪れてきた。
4. 酒の他にヨーグルトやアイスクリームのような製品も開発してきた。

● **Newspaper English**

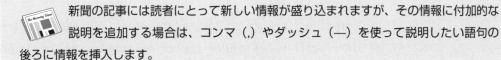

新聞の記事には読者にとって新しい情報が盛り込まれますが、その情報に付加的な説明を追加する場合は、コンマ（,）やダッシュ（—）を使って説明したい語句の後ろに情報を挿入します。

以下の1〜3の英文の（　　）内に入る追加情報をa〜cから選びましょう。

1. The two women — (　　　) — are now working as apprentices.
2. Nishiyama Shuzojo Co., (　　　), has tried to modernize its company practices.
3. Kaminsky, (　　　), joined the firm in August 2017.

    a. a former bartender and English teacher
    b. American Kelley Kaminsky, 28, and Chen Hsiao-jou, 26, from Taiwan
    c. known worldwide by sake connoisseurs for its award-winning Kotsuzumi brands

bring ideas to the table 「ア イデアを提供する」

Foreign pair bring energy and fresh ideas to the table in Japan's traditional sake industry

TAMBA, HYOGO PREF. — When two foreign nationals dipped their toe into the traditional sake brewing industry as sales staff, they not only discovered the intricacies of the beverage, but they also came to understand the unique aspects of working in one of the country's most traditional ₅ industries.

dip one's toe into... 「〜に足を踏み入れる」

The two women — American Kelley Kaminsky, 28, and Chen Hsiao-jou, 26, from Taiwan — are now working as apprentices to learn the ins and outs of sake brewing from a producer with a more than 160-year history in Hyogo ₁₀ Prefecture.

ins and outs 「ノウハウ」

Nishiyama Shuzojo Co., known worldwide by sake connoisseurs for its award-winning Kotsuzumi brands, has tried to modernize its company practices to respond to the decline in the consumption of alcohol in Japan, including by ₁₅ hiring women and foreign nationals at its *kura* (brewery) from around 2013.

connoisseur 「目利き」

"I wanted my *kura* to be a model in a declining industry by showing that we could change so much if we question tradition," said Shuzo Nishiyama, 45, the sixth-generation ₂₀ chief of Nishiyama Shuzojo.

sixth-generation chief 「6代目」

brewer 「杜氏（酒造りの職人）」

Currently, four out of seven Nishiyama Shuzojo brewers are women, and the president said female "attentiveness" helps in keeping accurate records of each brewing process, among other benefits. ₂₅

among other benefits 「他の利点の中でも」

Kaminsky, a former bartender and English teacher, joined the firm in August 2017, while Chen started working there in April after leaving a mushroom farm in Taiwan.

Sake is produced by mixing processed rice with water, *kōji* mold and sake yeast. The two foreign nationals, both fluent ₃₀ in Japanese, take part in almost every step of the process, including preparing *kōji*, mixing the ingredients and

mold 「菌」

yeast 「酵母」

ingredient 「材料」

recording the temperature of the sake at each step.

Nishiyama Shuzojo staff begin their day by cleaning their main workspace. At 8:30 a.m. all staff members gather outside to take part in calisthenics exercises, led by a
5 rotating cast of employees.

by a rotating cast of
employees「従業員が順番で」

Both Kaminsky and Chen said they were "surprised" by the cleaning and exercise programs at first.

"I think some people would leave the company for this in Taiwan," said a laughing Chen. "I thought 'this has nothing
10 to do with the work,' but I got used to it. That's what culture is. ... By doing it, you feel that you are actually in the culture."

Kyodo

● **Summary**   ◎ CD1-09

以下の空所 1 ～ 4 に当てはまる語を選択肢から選び、書き入れましょう。

Despite the sake industry's traditional image, one Hyogo-based producer is aiming to challenge the (1.   ) by diversifying its workforce. As part of this (2.   ), it has hired more women and foreign nationals as apprentice sake makers. While two non-Japanese female apprentices were initially surprised by some of the practices at their new (3.   ), the company chief praised the (4.   ) to detail that women seemed to bring to their work.

| workplace | stereotype | effort | attention |

以下の１～５の英文が本文の内容と合っていればＴ（True）、合っていなければＦ（False）
を（　　　）内に書き入れましょう。

1. Kaminsky and Chen had no experience in brewing sake before. （　　　）
2. Kaminsky and Chen are both in their 20s. （　　　）
3. Nishiyama Shuzojo was founded over 160 years ago. （　　　）
4. The staff members of the company are all women except the president. （　　　）
5. The employees start the day by cleaning and doing exercises. （　　　）

本文の内容に合うように、１の質問の答えとして適当なものを、２と３の英文を完成させ
るのに適当なものをａ～ｄから選びましょう。

1. What motivated Nishiyama Shuzojo Co. to change some of its working
   practices?
   a. Difficulty in finding men who were willing to do the hard work
   b. Falling numbers of Japanese people buying their products
   c. A desire to enter foreign markets for the first time
   d. A woman taking over as the head of the family-owned company

2. According to the article, part of the foreign workers' job includes
   a. combining the substances used to make sake.
   b. purchasing the mold used in the process.
   c. creating marketing campaigns for America and Taiwan.
   d. extracting special enzymes from mushrooms.

3. The company employees take it in turns to
   a. practice English with Kaminsky.
   b. teach their foreign coworkers Japanese.
   c. clean each other's work stations.
   d. lead the daily morning exercises.

The Yomiuri Shimbun

● Key Expressions 1

写真に関する音声を聞いて 1 ～ 3 の（　）内に適当な語を書き入れましょう。

1. Yoshiteru Mizuguchi, left, is a 79-year-old volunteer guide for the Kujukushima Pearl Sea Resort, a marine complex (o _ _ _ _ _ _ _) by Sasebo city.

水口良照さん（左の写真の左端の人物）は、佐世保市が運営する海洋総合施設「九十九島パールシーリゾート」の 79 歳のボランティア・ガイドである。

2. He uses pictures he took himself on one of his (t _ _ _ _) of the Kujukushima islands in Nagasaki Prefecture.

彼は長崎県の九十九島観光ツアーの一つで、自身が撮影した写真を（案内に）使用している。

3. He has become popular with tourists for the unique names he gives to the islands and their strange rock (f _ _ _ _ _ _ _ _ _), including "Merlion" in the picture on the right.

彼は、右の写真に写っている「マーライオン」など、（九十九島の）島々やそれらの島の奇妙な岩の姿に独特の名前を付けて、観光客に人気となっている。

● Key Expressions 2

接尾辞 -ion, -ation は、動詞の語尾について抽象名詞を形成します。-ion は「行為、状態」を、-ation は「行為、結果、（行為の結果生じた）状態」などの意味を表します。

枠内の説明を参考に、以下の 1 〜 7 の動詞に接尾辞をつけ、日本語の意味に合う名詞に変化させましょう。

1. form（形成する）　　　→ [　　　　　　　　　　　　　] （姿、構成、構造）

2. express（表現する）　→ [　　　　　　　　　　　　　] （表現、表情）

3. vary（変化する）　　　→ [　　　　　　　　　　　　　] （変化、変種）

4. react（反応する）　　　→ [　　　　　　　　　　　　　] （反応）

5. observe（観察する）　→ [　　　　　　　　　　　　　] （観察）

6. explain（説明する）　→ [　　　　　　　　　　　　　] （説明）

7. impress（印象を与える）→ [　　　　　　　　　　　　　] （印象）

● Key Expressions 3

分詞構文とは副詞節の代用で、主節を修飾する働きをする構文です。日本語訳を参考に、以下の 1 〜 3 の英文の（　　）内の動詞を現在分詞（V-ing）か過去分詞（V-ed）に変化させて、分詞構文を作りましょう。

1. (Point → 　　　　　　　　　　) to a fanciful rock formation sticking out into the blue sea, he guided a tour around rocky areas.
青い海に突き出た奇岩を指さしながら、彼は岩場を巡る観光案内ツアーを行った。

2. (Hail → 　　　　　　　　　　) from Nagahama, Shiga Prefecture, Mizuguchi worked as a sales clerk for a department store in Yokohama for about 40 years.
滋賀県長浜市出身の水口さんは、およそ 40 年間、横浜市にある百貨店の店員として勤務した。

3. (Attract → 　　　　　　　　　　) by the beautiful scenery of the Kujukushima islands, he became a volunteer guide in 2003.
彼は、九十九島の美しい景色に引きつけられて、2003 年にボランティア・ガイドとなった。

ボランティア観光ガイドの水口さんについて、英文に述べられているものを1〜4から選びましょう。

Mizuguchi has been commended by the Environment Ministry, the Sasebo city government and other entities for his unique tours. He even has fans who repeatedly join his tours, bringing along souvenirs to show their appreciation. Also, with the recent rapid increase in foreign cruise ships calling at Sasebo Port, Mizuguchi has taken a direct approach to promotion, arming himself with a poster featuring his own photos in an effort to show tourists the beauty of the islands he loves. He will turn 80 next year, but he has not lost his enthusiasm.

Notes   entity「団体」   appreciation「感謝」   arm oneself with...「〜で武装する」

The Japan News

1. 環境省など、複数の団体から表彰された。
2. 感謝の印として、観光客にお土産を渡すことにしている。
3. 観光案内の功績で、正社員に昇進することになった。
4. 80歳を区切りに、ガイドを引退することにしている。

● Newspaper English

たとえばa good-looking man「見た目のよい男性」、a Tokyo-based company「東京を拠点とする会社」などのようなハイフン付きの形容詞は、豊富な情報を簡潔に伝えるのに適しています。名詞がハイフン付きの形容詞を伴うことで切れ味のよい表現が生まれ、新聞記事でもしばしば用いられます。

以下の1と2の英文のペアがほぼ同じ意味になるように、(　　　)内にハイフン付きの形容詞を書き入れましょう。

1. He noticed there were a lot of rocks which looked strange.
=He noticed there were a lot of (　　　　　　　　　　　) rocks.
彼は奇妙な姿をした多くの岩があるのに気づいた。

2. In 2018 Kujukushima was added to the Most Beautiful Bays in the World Club, which is a nongovernmental organization based in France.
= In 2018 Kujukushima was added to the Most Beautiful Bays in the World Club, a (　　　　　　　　　　　) nongovernmental organization.
九十九島は2018年に、フランスを拠点とした非政府組織「世界で最も美しい湾クラブ」に仲間入りした。

'Rock star' guide offers boat tours of fanciful formations

"Everybody, that is Fukuro [owl] rock. It's a work of art created by nature," said pleasure boat guide Yoshiteru Mizuguchi, 79, as he pointed to a rocky area sticking out into the blue sea. Passengers aboard the boat, the "Pearl Queen," exclaimed, "It's the spitting image!" ⁵

Mizuguchi is a guide for the Kujukushima Pearl Sea Resort, a city-run marine complex including an aquarium, restaurants and souvenir shops in Sasebo, Nagasaki Prefecture. He has become popular with tourists for the unique names he gives to the Kujukushima islands and their ¹⁰ strange rock formations resembling animals and other creatures — so popular, in fact, that this May he gave the 7,000th tour of his 15-year career.

He has so far named about 30 rocks, including "Merlion", (named after the Singaporean mascot), "Nemuru Komainu" ¹⁵ (sleeping guardian dog) and the fanciful "Ago no Hazureta Monster" (monster with a dislocated jaw). He even names some formations after anime characters.

Hailing from Nagahama, Shiga Prefecture, Mizuguchi worked as a sales clerk for a department store in Yokohama ²⁰ for about 40 years before moving to Sasebo, where his wife's parents had a house. Attracted by the beautiful scenery of the Kujukushima islands — a chain of more than 200 islets both large and small — he became a volunteer guide in August 2003. He currently conducts tours 50 times a month. ²⁵

He got the idea to offer tours of the islands' strange-looking rocks about two years after starting as a volunteer guide, when he noticed one day that rocky areas resembling human faces would change from "the peaceful expression of a Buddha" to "a furious expression of a demon" depending on ³⁰ variations in light and shade. When he told passengers on the pleasure boat about his discovery, he was struck by the

pleasure boat 「遊覧船」

exclaim 「叫ぶ」

spitting image 「そっくり、生き写し」

aquarium 「水族館」

islet 「小島」

currently 「現在」

furious 「怒り狂った」

depending on... 「〜次第で」

greater-than-expected reaction to his observation from passengers both young and old.

greater-than-expected「期待以上の」

"Although passengers easily tire of difficult historical theories, everyone can enjoy the shapes of rock formations right before them and also have fun searching out new ones themselves," Mizuguchi said. "Rather than one-way, boring tours, explanations with interesting names leave an impression because they're something anyone can enjoy," he added.

The Japan News

● Summary

以下の空所 1 〜 4 に当てはまる語を選択肢から選び、書き入れましょう。

A volunteer tour guide has proven to be a big (1.   ) among tourists thanks to his talent for giving memorable names to the local scenery. Retiree Yoshiteru Mizuguchi has been conducting tours of the Kujukushima islands in Nagasaki Prefecture for 15 years since moving to the (2.   ) from Yokohama. He thinks that one reason for the (3.   ) of his memorable tours is the unusual names he has given to various rock formations and islands based on their (4.   ) according to the light conditions.

| hit | area | appearance | popularity |

以下の英文の（　　）内に当てはまる形容詞を選択肢からすべて選び○で囲みましょう。

Mizuguchi has succeeded in offering everyone (   ) tours.

| boring   interactive   tiring   furious |
| economical   historical   enjoyable |

本文の内容に合うように、1と3の英文を完成させるのに適当なものを、2の質問の答えとして適当なものをa〜dから選びましょう。

1. One of the names given to the rocks by Mizuguchi is inspired by
   a. a famous landmark in a foreign country.
   b. a famous queen from the region who loved pearls.
   c. a well-known shop for tourists in Sasebo.
   d. a favorite dog his family owned in Yokohama.

2. Which of the following is biggest?
   a. The number of years Mizuguchi has lived in Sasebo
   b. The number of tours Mizuguchi gives per month
   c. The number of rocks Mizuguchi has named
   d. The number of years Mizuguchi worked as a sales clerk

3. Mizuguchi thinks that people
   a. enjoy the challenge of remembering over 200 island names.
   b. find his non-local accent to be pleasantly unusual.
   c. prefer one-way tours because they never see the same thing twice.
   d. often get bored when listening to difficult historical explanations.

Chapter 4

A Banana with an Edible Peel

国産バナナの救世主

The Asahi Shimbun

● Key Expressions 1

CD1-14

音声を聞いて1～3の（　　）内に適当な語を書き入れましょう。

1. In Japan and the US, more bananas are (c _ _ _ _ _ _ _) than any other fruit.
   日本とアメリカ合衆国においては、他のどの果物よりもバナナの消費量が多い。

2. A strain of banana was developed by an Okayama farm to (w _ _ _ _ _ _ _ _)
   the Japanese winter.
   あるバナナ種が、日本の冬に耐えられるように、岡山のある農場で開発された。

3. The company is now preparing to (s _ _ _) the crop to large cities in the
   Kansai and Kanto regions.
   その会社は現在、関西・関東地区の大都市にその農作物を出荷する準備を進めている。

● Key Expressions 2

-able, -ible は「～することが可能である」や「～することに適している」という意味を表す接尾辞です。こうした接尾辞を持つ形容詞は、もとになっている動詞にこれらの意味をプラスした意味を持ちます。また、接尾辞がつくことで元の動詞の形が変わる場合もあるので注意が必要です。

枠内の接尾辞の説明を参考に、以下の 1 ～ 5 の動詞を形容詞に書きかえましょう。

1. eat（食べる）　　　　→[　　　　　　　　　]（食べられる）
2. remove（取り外す）　→[　　　　　　　　　]（取り外せる）
3. wear（身につける）　→[　　　　　　　　　]（身につけられる）
4. adjust（調節する）　→[　　　　　　　　　]（調節できる）
5. use（使用する）　　　→[　　　　　　　　　]（使用できる）

● Key Expressions 3

日本語訳を参考に、以下の 1 ～ 3 の英文の（　　）内に当てはまる語句を選択肢から選び、書き入れましょう。

1. The Cavendish variety is (　　　　　　　　　　　) from a global epidemic of a new strain of Panama disease.
   キャベンディッシュ種は、新パナマ病の世界的流行の脅威にさらされている。

2. A new banana farm is now (　　　　　　　　　　) in Okayama Prefecture.
   新しいバナナ農場が現在岡山県で建設中である。

3. A new method of freezing the seeds and seedlings is (　　　　　　　　　).
   種子と種苗の新しい冷凍方法が検討されている。

| under consideration | under construction | under threat |

● Background Knowledge

 CD1-15

新種のバナナの栽培を始めた企業について、英文に述べられているものを 1 〜 4 から選び
ましょう。

Akio Uchida, president of Fukuoka-based construction company Next
Engineering Co., is banking on bananas for his company's future. The primary
business of his company is drainage works, but sales have dwindled. Uchida
explained that once a sewage system is installed, there is little else to do other
than occasional maintenance.

As his parents, who used to grow rice, were getting on in years, their rice
paddies generally remained uncultivated. It was while Uchida was exploring how
to put the land to good use that he learned about the premium "made-in-Japan"
banana.

The Asahi Shimbun

Notes　bank on... 「〜に賭ける、〜を頼みにする」　　drainage work 「下水道工事」　　get on in years
「だんだん年をとる」

1. バナナ栽培だけを行う子会社を設立した。
2. 下水道工事の仕事は現在も順調に利益を伸ばしている。
3. 長年稲作を営んできた内田社長の両親がバナナ栽培を提案した。
4. 内田社長は耕作放棄地となっていた土地を活用する方法を模索していた。

● Newspaper English

if だけでなく、given that... 「〜ということを考慮すると、〜と仮定すると」や
provided [providing] that... 「〜という条件で、〜の場合に限って」なども条
件・仮定の表現として、しばしば用いられます。それぞれの特徴を理解し、活用しましょう。

日本語訳を参考に、以下の 1 と 2 の英文の（　　）内に given か provided [providing] の
どちらかより相応しいほうを書き入れましょう。

1. (　　　　　　　　　) that organic bananas go for 800 yen and up a pop, a
single banana plant has the potential to produce 120,000 yen's worth of fruit.
有機バナナが 1 本 800 円以上で売られることを考慮すれば、1 株のバナナで 12 万
円相当の価値を生み出す可能性がある。

2. You can withdraw up to 500,000 yen a day at ATMs, (　　　　　　　　)
that you have sufficient money in your account.
口座に十分な現金がある場合に限り、ATM で 1 日 50 万円まで引き出せる。

Banana with edible skin gaining popularity

Ayumi Matsumoto works for an agricultural corporation in Minami-Kyushu, Kagoshima Prefecture, that grows a strain of organic banana with a thin, edible skin. The strain was developed by an Okayama farm to withstand the Japanese winter. ₅

pesticide「（農業用）殺虫剤」

Organic bananas grown without the use of pesticides by Kami Banana, the company Matsumoto works for, have a thin skin and plump flesh. The skin can be eaten, and is tasty, even nutritious.

nutritious「栄養価が高い」

laborious「骨の折れる」

Farming bananas using non-pesticide methods is a ₁₀ laborious business. Matsumoto has to remove pests by hand, which is quite a challenge as he tends to 2,100 plants on a 1.3-hectare plot. Banana bunches are harvested just before they fall to the ground, when the flesh is at its best. Each plant yields between 120 and 150 bananas in a typical ₁₅ harvest. Given that organic bananas go for 800 yen and up a pop, a single banana plant has the potential to produce 120,000 yen worth of fruit.

banana bunch「バナナの房」
at one's best「1番よい状態で」

The variety grown by Kami Banana is a new strain of Gros Michel developed by D&T Farm Inc., based in Okayama. ₂₀ The tropical plants sold by D&T Farm are more cold-resistant because the seeds and seedlings are frozen at minus 60 degrees. The process, which is called "the freeze-thaw awakening method," dramatically speeds up the growth of the plants in this variable climate. ₂₅

variable「変化しやすい」

plantation「農園」

D&T Farm began marketing the strain in 2017. The farm organizes workshops for plantations that purchase the plants. Currently, the variety is grown by 16 farms in Japan, and interest is growing.

Today, more than 99 percent of bananas sold in Japan are ₃₀ imported from the Philippines and other nations with a similarly warm climate. Most are of the Cavendish variety, which is favored for its rich texture, but it is under threat

rich texture「濃厚な食感」

from a global epidemic of a new strain of Panama disease that kills banana plants.

It is said that the Cavendish banana might be difficult to come by in Japan in the future, and even if imported, its retail price would be prohibitive. If a single organic banana can fetch 800 yen, or even more, money might grow on trees.

prohibitive「法外な」

fetch...「～（ある値段）で売れる」

〈参考〉 the freeze-thaw awakening method「凍結解凍覚醒法」：植物の種子など
を凍結解凍することにより、潜在的な能力を呼び覚まし、耐寒性の優れた個体
を作り出す技術のこと。

The Asahi Shimbun

● Summary ◎ CD1-17

以下の空所1～4に当てはまる語を選択肢から選び、書き入れましょう。

A Japanese company has developed a revolutionary type of banana with a thin, edible (1.   ). Interest in these new bananas is growing as they have been specifically engineered for Japan's (2.   ) and can be sold individually for a high price. Their (3.   ) to farmers is further enhanced by the fact that the common Cavendish variety of banana is under threat from a new (4.   ).

| climate | appeal | peel | disease |

「皮まで食べられるバナナ」について、当てはまるものには T（True）を、当てはまらないものには F（False）を 1 ～ 4 の（　　）内に書き入れましょう。

1. It can survive cold weather and grow outside tropical or subtropical regions.

（　　）

2. It was developed based on the Cavendish. （　　）

3. Some growers remove pests by hand since no pesticides are used. （　　）

4. Its seeds and seedlings are frozen at minus 120 degrees. （　　）

本文の内容に合うように、1 ～ 3 の英文を完成させるのに適当なものを a ～ d から選びましょう。

1. Kami Banana
   a. was the first company to develop bananas with an edible peel.
   b. refrains from using chemicals to protect the banana plants from pests.
   c. is owned by a farming corporation based in Okayama.
   d. is managed by the person who first discovered edible banana peels.

2. Even the lowest-yielding plants grown by Kami Banana have the potential to produce fruit worth
   a. 2,100 yen.
   b. 80,000 yen.
   c. 96,000 yen.
   d. 120,000 yen.

3. Cavendish bananas have historically been popular because
   a. people like the texture of the variety.
   b. they are ideally suited to Japan's climate.
   c. they are grown exclusively in the Philippines.
   d. they are resistant to a new strain of Panama disease.

Chapter 5

Too Crowded to Carry it on our Backs!

バッグにまつわるお国事情

The Japan Times

● Key Expressions 1

CD1-18

音声を聞いて１～３の（　　）内に適当な語を書き入れましょう。

1. For several years, railways have been (u _ _ _ _ _) passengers to place their backpacks on baggage racks or carry them on their front.
数年の間、鉄道各社は、バックパックを荷棚に上げるか前に持つよう、乗客に促している。

2. Backpacks sometimes get in the way of people standing (b _ _ _ _ _) them and cause problems.
バックパックは時として後ろにいる人の邪魔になり、問題を引き起こす場合がある。

3. A bag manufacturer released a slim (r _ _ _ _ _ _ _ _ _ _) backpack designed to be worn on a person’s front.
あるバッグメーカーは、前に持つようデザインされたスリムな長方形のバックパックを発売した。

● Key Expressions 2

日本語の意味に合うように、以下の1〜5の語句を完成させるのに適当な動詞を選び、
（　　）内に書き入れましょう。

1. (　　　　　　　　　　) in the way of...　　　　　　［〜の邪魔をする］
2. (　　　　　　　　　　) up with promotional posters　　　［宣伝ポスターを思いつく］
3. (　　　　　　　　　　) onto a train　　　　　　　　　［電車に飛び乗る］
4. (　　　　　　　　　　) too much　　　　　　　　　　［膨らみすぎる］
5. (　　　　　　　　　　) a nuisance to...　　　　　　　［〜の迷惑になる］

be	rush	get	come	bulge

● Key Expressions 3

日本語訳を参考に、以下の1〜4の英文の（　　）内に適当な動詞を選択肢から選び、必
要なら形を変えて書き入れましょう。複数回使うものもあります。

1. Framed rucksacks are said to (　　　　　　　　　　　　) into use around the
   1930s.
   フレーム・リュックサックは1930年代あたりに用いられるようになったと言われ
   ている。

2. Backpacks are designed to (　　　　　　　　　　　　) on people's backs.
   バックパックは人の背中に背負うようデザインされている。

3. Balancing the weight on both shoulders makes it possible for people to
   (　　　　　　　　　　　) heavier loads.
   両肩で重さのバランスを取るので、より重い荷物を運ぶことが可能になる。

4. A bag manufacturer encourages people to hold their bags in ways that do not
   (　　　　　　　　　　　) problems for others.
   あるバッグメーカーは他の人の迷惑にならないやり方でバッグを持つよう人々に促
   している。

cause	carry	come

小田急電鉄のバックパックに関する対応について、英文に述べられているものを1〜4から選びましょう。

An Odakyu official said it has been using posters to urge people not to carry their backpacks behind them since at least fiscal 2005, in response to rush-hour incidents such as those bags getting stuck between closing doors and causing train delays, as well as trouble arising among passengers.

"We are asking passengers for their cooperation so that everyone can use our trains in a pleasant manner," the official said. "We feel there have been fewer incidents after putting up posters and having station attendants and conductors make announcements asking passengers to hold their bags in front."

The Japan Times

1. 小田急電鉄は10年以上もバックパックを持たないよう乗客に通告してきた。
2. ラッシュアワー時の混雑状況の軽減のためにバックパックへの注意喚起を行った。
3. ポスターを貼るという対応は、マナー改善に効果がないことがわかった。
4. 駅員や車掌がバックパックを前に持つようアナウンスを行っている。

● **Newspaper English**

 新聞では紙面が限られているため簡潔な表現が好まれ、省略できるものは省略される場合がよくあります。特に接続詞 when と while が用いられる節では、しばしば主語と be 動詞の省略が起こります。

以下の1と2の英文で省略されていると考えられる主語と動詞を、（　　）内に書き入れましょう。

1. Railway companies ask passengers to put their backpacks on baggage racks or carry them on their front when (　　　　　) (　　　　　) on crowded trains.
   鉄道各社は、満員電車に乗車中は、バックパックを荷棚に上げるか前に持つかするよう乗客に頼んでいる。

2. It is easy to take things out of the bag when (　　　　　) (　　　　　) carried in front.
   前に持つとカバンから物を取り出しやすい。

Back to front for manners on Japanese public transport

Backpacks, as the word suggests, are designed to be carried on people's backs. But there are a growing number of people in Japan who hold these bags in front, especially on trains and buses.

For several years, railways have been urging passengers 5 to place their backpacks on baggage racks or carry them on their front when on crowded trains to prevent the bags from getting in the way of people standing behind them, as the holders are often unaware of what is happening outside their field of vision. 10

The calls have become part of promotional activities to discourage bad manners while riding on trains and other forms of transportation in densely populated regions.

In urban areas, train conductors and station attendants make occasional announcements asking passengers to avoid 15 actions such as rushing onto trains, talking on their mobile phones and carrying their knapsacks on their back.

Operators serving the Kanto region, including the Tokyo Metropolitan Government's Bureau of Transportation, which runs the Toei subway and bus systems, and Odakyu Electric 20 Railway Co., have also come up with promotional posters and brochures that encourage users not to be a nuisance to others.

The move has even spread to the bag manufacturing industry, with Ace Co. releasing a slim rectangular backpack 25 designed to be worn on a person's front.

"Because more and more people are carrying rucksacks on trains and are becoming attentive to having good manners, we developed a backpack designed to be less obstructive inside trains," said Ayane Yamada, a public information 30 officer with Ace.

"The pockets are designed so it's easy to take things out of

the Tokyo Metropolitan Government's Bureau of Transportation 「東京都交通局」

Odakyu Electric Railway Co. 「小田急電鉄」

Ace Co. 「エース株式会社」

obstructive 「邪魔になる」
public information officer 「広報担当者」

the bag when it's carried in front, either on both shoulders or just on one side," she said. "Backpacks are generally thought of as bulky, with a large capacity, but this product is designed to have a relatively small width and doesn't bulge too much
5 even when you put things in it."

bulky「かさばる」

relatively「比較的」

Yamada said the bag-maker hopes to keep calling people's attention to holding their bags in ways that do not cause problems for others in places such as crowded trains.

The Japan Times

● Summary

 CD1-21

以下の空所1〜4に当てはまる語を選択肢から選び、書き入れましょう。ただし、文頭に来る語も小文字で与えられています。

As more and more people carry backpacks on Japan's public transport systems, an awareness of the nuisance they can be to other passengers is also (1.   ). In response to a number of promotional campaigns run by transport providers, many passengers are (2.   ) the problem by (3.   ) their bags on their front. (4.   ) this trend, a bag-maker has developed a rucksack specifically designed to be worn on the front.

carrying	solving	noticing	growing

本文の内容に合うように、以下の表にそれぞれの取り組みをまとめましょう。

鉄道会社の数年前からの取り組み	(1.　　　　　　　　　　　　　　　　　　　　) では、バックパックを (2.　　　　　　　　　　) か (3.　　　　　　　　　　) よう、乗客に促している。		
都市部での車掌・駅員の取り組み	(4.　　　　　　　　　　　　) や、(5.　　　　　　　　　　　　　　　　)、(6.　　　　　　　　　　　) ことといった行為を避けるよう乗客にお願いするアナウンスを時々行っている。		
関東の公共交通機関の取り組み	利用者に他の人の迷惑とならないことを促すために、(7.　　　　　　　　　　　) や (8.　　　　　　　　　　) を考案した。		

本文の内容に合うように、1の質問の答えとして適当なものを、2と3の英文を完成させるのに適当なものをa〜dから選びましょう。

1. Why can rucksacks sometimes be a nuisance when worn on the back?
   a. Wearers cannot see if their bag is in the way of others.
   b. They exert too much pressure on the wearer's shoulders.
   c. They often become smelly in crowded, hot train carriages.
   d. The size of the backpacks people are wearing is increasing.

2. One method used by train operators to encourage good manners is
   a. fining people who are discovered to be breaking the rules.
   b. having staff patrol the carriages and give warnings to passengers.
   c. making announcements via passengers' mobile phones.
   d. providing various printed materials detailing good manners.

3. According to the article, Ace's new backpack features
   a. just one small pocket designed to hold essential items.
   b. a number of safety features that deter pickpockets.
   c. a design that allows it to be worn in various ways.
   d. one of the largest capacities on the market.

Chapter *6*

Monitoring Kid's Phone Use

使わせる？使わせない？

Aflo

● **Key Expressions 1**　　　　　　　　　　　　　　　◎ CD1-22

写真に関する音声を聞いて 1 ～ 3 の（　　）内に適当な語を書き入れましょう。

1. In their Chicago apartment, Jennea Bivens, left, talks with her 13-year-old daughter, Ayrial Miller, about the contacts in her social media (a _ _ _ _ _ _).
   ジェニア・ビベンズさん（左）が、シカゴのアパートで13歳の娘アリエル・ミラーさんと、ソーシャルメディアのアカウントでのやりとりについて話をしている。

2. (E _ _ _ _ _ _) to tablets and smartphones at an increasingly early age, kids are savvier about using them and share tips with friends.
   タブレットやスマートフォンにますます幼い年齢でさらされるようになって、子どもたちはそれらをよりうまく使いこなし、友達と秘密情報を共有する。

3. Parents, by (c _ _ _ _ _ _ _), are often naive about what their kids can do with those devices.
   逆に、親たちは、子どもたちがそれらの端末で何ができるかについてしばしば分かっていないことがある。

英語の話し言葉では wanna のような短縮表現がしばしば使われます。これは want to の略で、特にアメリカ英語でよく聞かれる表現です。書き言葉では、発言を直接引用するときなどに見られます。

以下の 1 〜 4 の英文の下線部の省略形を、元の形に書きかえましょう。

1. I gotta go now. → (　　　　　　　　　　　　) go now.

2. I'm gonna share it with her. → I'm (　　　　　　　　　　) share it with her.

3. Lemme have a look at it. → (　　　　　　　　　　) have a look at it.

4. Sorry, I dunno for sure. → Sorry, I (　　　　　　　　　) for sure.

否定の意味を持つ副詞や only を伴う副詞句が文頭に来るとき、後に続く主語と動詞が逆になって倒置が起こることがあります。そのほか、仮定法の if が省略されたときにも倒置が起こります。

以下の 1 〜 3 の英文の下線部に注意して、日本語訳を完成させましょう。

1. She makes no apology. Nor should she, said a retired cybercrimes detective who spoke to her.
彼女は謝らない。(　　　　　　　　　　　　　　　)、と彼女に話しかけた元ネット犯罪捜査官は言った。

2. Only recently did her mother start a live video stream on Twitter.
(　　　　　　　　　　　　　) 彼女の母親は、ツィッターのライブオンライン動画発信を始めた。

3. Should the situation change, parents will have to monitor their children's phone use around the clock.
(　　　　　　　　　　　　　)、親たちは一日中子どもたちの携帯電話使用を監視しなければならなくなるだろう。

子どもたちのソーシャルメディア利用について、英文に述べられているものを１～４から選びましょう。

A 2016 Pew Research Center survey found that only about half of parents said they had ever checked their children's phone calls and text messages or even friended their kids on social media.

Tech experts agree that monitoring makes sense for younger kids. Rich Wistocki, a retired detective, tells parents to offer their children the promise of no punishment when they come to them about mistakes they have made online or help they need with a social media problem.

The Associated Press

Notes　friend... 「～を（SNSの）友達リストに加える」　punishment「罰」

1. ある調査によると、子どもたちのソーシャルメディア利用には、ほとんどの親が全く関心を持っていない。
2. ある調査によると、子どもたちのソーシャルメディア上の付き合いを奨励している親が多い。
3. 専門家たちは幼い子どもたちのソーシャルメディア利用を監視してもよいと思っている。
4. ある元捜査官は、子どもたちのオンライン上での間違った行動は厳しく罰するべきだと述べている。

● **Newspaper English**

新聞記事中では同じ表現を繰り返すことを避ける傾向にあります。例えば、「幸せな生活を送る」という表現は、live/lead a happy life という表現がありますが、こうした同意表現を利用して言い換えていくのは新聞記事の重要な手法です。

以下の英文の１と２の（　　）内の動詞を適当な形に変化させましょう。

Although many teens themselves say it is surprisingly common for kids (¹· live→　　　　　　) online lives that are all but invisible to most parents, few parents worry about the secret digital lives their children are (²· lead →　　　　　).

子どもたちが、ほとんどの親にはほぼ見えていないのも同然のオンライン生活を送っているのは驚くほど一般的なことだと、多くの十代の子どもたち自身が語っているが、子どもたちが送っている秘密のデジタル生活について心配している親は少ない。

Do you know what your kid's doing on their phone?

be annoyed「イライラしている」
couch「ソファ」
aka「すなわち」

narrow to a surly squint「不機嫌そうに細められる」

K-8 public school「小中一貫の公立学校」

dreadful array of consequences「恐ろしい数々の影響」
occasional「時折起こる」
risqué「きわどい」
burner phone「使い捨て携帯」

gotta...「〜せねばならない」
hand it to...「〜を評価する」

academics「学者」

CHICAGO — Ayrial Miller is clearly annoyed. Her mother is sitting with her on the couch in their Chicago apartment, scrolling through the teen's contacts on social media.

"Who's this?" asks Jennea Bivens, aka Mom.

"It's a friend of a friend," Ayrial says. They have not talked 5 online in a while.

"Delete it," her mom says.

The 13-year-old's eyes narrow to a surly squint. "I hate this! I hate this! I hate this!" she shouts.

Yes, Bivens admits she is one of "those moms." She makes 10 no apology.

Nor should she, said Rich Wistocki, a retired cybercrimes detective who spoke to her and other parents in early June at Nathan Hale Elementary School, a K-8 public school in Chicago. 15

"There is no such thing as privacy for children," Wistocki told them.

Other tech experts might disagree. But even they worry about the secret digital lives many teens are leading, and the dreadful array of consequences — including harassment and 20 occasional suicides — that can result.

Today's kids are meeting strangers, some of them adults, on a variety of apps. Teens are storing risqué photos in vault apps, and then trading those photos like baseball cards.

Some even have spare "burner" phones to avoid parental 25 monitoring.

"I gotta hand it to their creativity, but it's only enabled through technology," says David Coffey, a dad and tech expert from Cadillac, Mich.

It is difficult to say how many kids are pushing digital 30 boundaries this way. But academics, experts like Wistocki and Coffey, and many teens themselves say it is surprisingly common for kids to live online lives that are all but invisible to most parents.　And yet, Wistocki says, too often parents remain in denial with what he calls "NMK — not my kid."

and yet「それでもなお」

in denial「現実から目をそらしている」

Ayrial's mom uses an app called MMGuardian, one of several available, to manage and monitor her 13-year-old daughter's phone use. She turns off certain apps, sometimes as punishment, and monitors texts.

"It's a full-time job," Bivens concedes. "People laugh at me because I monitor her stuff. But I don't have the same problems as other people do."

concede「認める」

〈参考〉vault　apps：見られたくないデータを隠すプライバシー保護のためのAndroid アプリ。写真や動画のほか、連絡先や通話記録、その他アプリなどにパスワードをかけてロックすることができる。

The Associated Press

● Summary　　　　　　　　　　　　　　　　　　　　　　　　◎ CD1-25

以下の空所１〜４に当てはまる語を選択肢から選び、書き入れましょう。

Thanks to advances in technology, young children and teens may be living online (**1.**　　　　　　　　　) of which their parents are unaware. This can leave young people at risk from increased exposure to (**2.**　　　　　　　　　), bullying and even suicide. Though some children may protest, some tech (**3.**　　　　　　　　　) advocate that parents monitor their children's online behavior much more closely, even going so far as to suggest that children should not have any privacy when it comes to their online (**4.**　　　　　　　　　).

strangers　　experts　　interactions　　lives

以下の１～４について、ビベンズさんがとるであろう行動と推測できるものを１つ選びましょう。

1. She will hate going through her daughter's contacts in her social media account.

2. If she finds suspicious emails sent to her daughter, she will end the connection quickly.

3. She will advise her daughter to use a vault app.

4. She will not care about her daughter's wrongful use of social media.

本文の内容に合うように、１と３の英文を完成させるのに適当なものを、２の質問の答えとして適当なものをａ～ｄから選びましょう。

1. Ayrial Miller finds her mother's monitoring of her online activity
   a. understandable.
   b. boring.
   c. friendly.
   d. irritating.

2. Which of the following best describes Rich Wistocki?
   a. A retiree who advises parents of young children
   b. A cybercrime expert who found a way to unlock vault apps
   c. An elementary school teacher who is concerned about his students
   d. An advocate for the protection of children's rights to privacy

3. Wistocki believes part of the problem is that some parents
   a. do not understand how to use monitoring apps.
   b. are giving children their own phones at too young an age.
   c. fail to realize that their own children could be at risk.
   d. are just as addicted to online apps as their kids.

Chapter 7

Learn about your Pet Dog at the Museum

ワンコの歴史

AFP/JIJI

● **Key Expressions 1**   ◎ CD1-26

音声を聞いて1〜3の（　）内に適当な語を書き入れましょう。

1. The American Kennel Club Museum of the Dog (o _ _ _ _ _) in midtown Manhattan, NY.

アメリカンケネルクラブ（米国愛犬家団体）の犬の博物館がニューヨーク市マンハッタンのミッドタウンにオープンした。

2. This museum returned to New York after three (d _ _ _ _ _ _) on the outskirts of St. Louis.

この博物館は、30年間（ミズーリ州）セントルイス郊外にあったが、そののちニューヨークに戻ってきた。

3. The exhibition (r _ _ _ _ _) from the scientific to the whimsical.

展示品は科学的なものから風変わりなものまで多岐にわたる。

以下の１〜７は博物館や学術調査に関する語句です。日本語訳を選択肢から選び、（　　）内に書き入れましょう。

1. artifact　　　　　　　　（　　　　　　　　　）
2. fossil　　　　　　　　　（　　　　　　　　　）
3. curator　　　　　　　　（　　　　　　　　　）
4. extensive collection　　（　　　　　　　　）コレクション
5. donated collection　　　（　　　　　　　　）コレクション
6. appraiser　　　　　　　（　　　　　　　　　）
7. peruse　　　　　　　　（　　　　　　　　　）

学芸員　　　鑑定人　　　人工遺物　　　閲覧する　　　化石　　　寄贈の　　　多数の

以下の１〜４の英文の（　　）内に当てはまる語を選択肢から選び、書き入れましょう。

1. Some devices let people (　　　　　　　　) their hand at basic dog training with a virtual puppy.
   ヴァーチャル子犬で基本的な犬のしつけを試しにやらせる機器もある。

2. There are some just-don't-knows, but the collection is (　　　　　　　　) on purebreds.
   知らない犬種もあるが、コレクションは純血種に焦点が当てられている。

3. The main point to take away is the fact that dogs were (　　　　　　　　) to have different jobs.
   （これらのコレクションから）引き出せる主な点は、犬は様々な仕事をするように意図されていたという事実である。

4. Visitors can no longer (　　　　　　　　) their own pet pooches. And admission rates are higher: $15 for most adults in New York, compared to $6 in St. Louis.
   訪問客はもう自分のペットのワンちゃんを連れて来られない。また入場料も高くなっており、セントルイスでは 6 ドルだったのに比べ、ニューヨークでは、ほとんどの大人は 15 ドルである。

bring　　　focused　　　try　　　meant

アメリカンケネルクラブの犬の博物館について、英文に<u>述べられていないもの</u>を 1 〜 4 から選びましょう。

　　The American Kennel Club Museum of the Dog opened in the kennel club's New York headquarters in 1982. Seeking more space and hoping to attract more than its roughly 15,000 annual visitors, the museum moved in 1987 to a historic house owned by St. Louis County.

　　Another planned move, to a new development in a nearby city, did not materialize. Neither did the hoped-for attendance boost: the museum counted under 10,000 visitors last year.

The Associated Press

Note　　county「郡」

1. この博物館は最初ニューヨークにあった。
2. セントルイスに移転してから訪問客が急激に増えた。
3. その後の移転の計画は実現しなかった。
4. 昨年の訪問者数は 10,000 人を割った。

● **Newspaper English**

　新聞のヘッドラインでは、簡潔で興味を引く表現で読者を惹きつける工夫がなされます。<u>be 動詞や冠詞の省略</u>や、<u>記事を新鮮に見せるため過去のことも現在形で表す</u>ほかに、<u>未来は不定詞（to V）で表す</u>といったいくつかのルールがあります。

枠内の説明と日本語訳を参考に、以下の 1 〜 3 の（　　）内の動詞を適当な形にし、ヘッドラインを完成させましょう。

1. New dog museum (unleash →　　　　　　　　　) in New York City
   新しい犬の博物館がニューヨーク市に「放たれる」　　 ***Note:*** leash「革ひもでつなぐ」

2. Dog museum (open →　　　　　　　　　) in NY
   犬の博物館、ニューヨークにオープンの予定

3. Kennel Club (attract →　　　　　　　　　) visitors to new dog museum
   ケネルクラブ、新たな犬の博物館に訪問客を惹きつけている

New dog museum unleashed in New York City

NEW YORK — This museum invites visitors to come! Sit! And stay!

The American Kennel Club Museum of the Dog opens Feb. 8 in midtown Manhattan, returning to New York after three decades on the outskirts of St. Louis. ⁵

The collection boasts portraits of royal and presidential pets, artifacts that trace canine history as far back as an estimated 30 million-year-old fossil, and devices that "match" visitors' faces with dog breeds and let people try their hand at basic dog training with a virtual puppy. ¹⁰

While there won't be actual dogs except for special occasions, the museum hopes to give visitors "an understanding of the history of dogs, how they came to be in such different variety," said Executive Director Alan Fausel, a longtime art curator and appraiser seen on PBS's "Antiques ¹⁵ Roadshow."

About 150 pieces from the kennel club's extensive, mostly donated collection are on view at the museum, which also has a library area for perusing some of the club's 15,000 books.

Fanciers will find images and information on canines from ²⁰ bulldogs to borzois to Bedlington terriers. There are some just-don't-knows, but the collection is focused on purebreds.

The kennel club, which runs the nation's oldest purebred dog registry, has taken heat over the years from animal-welfare activists who view dog breeding as a beauty contest ²⁵ that fuels puppy mills. The club argues there is value in breeding to hone various traits, from companionability to bomb-sniffing acumen, and hopes the museum helps make the case.

"I think the main point to take away is the fact that dogs ³⁰ were meant to have different jobs," Fausel said. "It's learning why they were purposely bred for certain jobs, and their activities and their attributes."

boast... 「～を誇る」

royal 「王室の」

canine 「犬の」

PBS＝米国のテレビ局

fancier 「(犬の) 愛好家」

registry 「登記」

take heat 「批判を受ける」

animal-welfare activist 「動物愛護活動家」

puppy mill 「パピーミル (子犬工場)」

hone... 「～を研ぎ澄ませる」

companionability 「人になつく性質」

acumen 「鋭敏な能力」

make the case 「(ある立場を) 弁護する」

The exhibition ranges from the scientific — such as a 19th-century skeleton representing an important stage in the evolution of the smooth fox terrier — to the whimsical, including one of photographer William Wegman's images of
5 Weimaraners in humanlike situations (in this case, canoeing). There is also a tiny, elaborate, Edwardian-style dog house for a Chihuahua, and a wall of movie posters celebrating canine stars from "Lassie" to "Beethoven."

purposely「意図的に」
attribute「特性」

elaborate「精巧な」
Edwardian「エドワード朝の」

〈参考〉Weimaraner「ワイマラナー（狩猟犬の一種）」：19 世紀に作られたドイツ原
産の大型の狩猟犬。万能な狩猟犬を目指して徹底的に改良が重ねられた。主に
ドイツ国内で王族に利用されたのち、アメリカやイギリスにも輸出され、人気
を博している。

The Associated Press

● Summary   ◉ CD1-29

以下の空所 1 〜 4 に当てはまる語を選択肢から選び、書き入れましょう。

A museum about dogs has been relocated to New York in the United States. Run by the American Kennel Club, it mainly focuses on (1.   ) dogs, although the practice of (2.   ) dog breeding has been criticized by some. Visitors to the museum will find a wide range of exhibits, from (3.   ) explanations of the evolution of various breeds, to lighter, interactive sections and posters and portraits of (4.   ) canines.

| selective | famous | scientific | purebred |

本文の内容に合うように、以下の表の情報をまとめましょう。

The number of items on exhibit in the Dog Museum	About (¹.) pieces
The number of books owned by the Kennel Club	(².) books
Examples of exhibits	・a (³.)-year-old fossil ・Devices that match visitors' faces with (⁴.) ・Devices that let people try their hand at basic dog training with (⁵.)

本文の内容に合うように、1の質問の答えとして適当なものを、2と3の英文を完成させるのに適当なものをa〜dから選びましょう。

1. For how many years was the museum located outside of New York?
   a. 3 years
   b. 8 years
   c. 10 years
   d. 30 years

2. The museum accumulated the objects in its collection mainly through
   a. gifts from the original owners.
   b. discoveries made by Alan Fausel.
   c. the sale of thousands of books.
   d. other museums.

3. Visitors to the museum will be able to find
   a. a live smooth fox terrier, the museum's living mascot.
   b. an ancient canoe, decorated with pictures of dogs.
   c. a very small house that was designed for a pet.
   d. a wall of paintings depicting famous people.

Chapter 8

Dream of Space Tourism Comes True

新時代のゴールドラッシュ

AFP PHOTO / VIRGIN GALACTIC

● **Key Expressions 1**　　　　　　　　　　　　　　　◎ CD1-30

音声を聞いて1〜3の（　　）内に適当な語を書き入れましょう。

1. Virgin Galactic is (l _ _ _ _ _ _) the pack in the pursuit of space tourism.
   ヴァージン・ギャラクティック社は、宇宙旅行計画の追求において先頭に立っている。

2. Richard Branson, the (f _ _ _ _ _ _) of Virgin Galactic, hoped to be one of the first passengers in the next 12 months.
   ヴァージン・ギャラクティック社の創設者のリチャード・ブランソン氏は、1年後には自身が最初の乗客の一人になりたいと思っていた。

3. During a May 29 test in California's Mojave Desert, the spaceship exceeded an (a _ _ _ _ _ _ _ _) of 21 miles (34 km), heading for space.
   カリフォルニア州のモハーベ砂漠で行った5月29日のテスト中に、宇宙船は高度21マイル（34キロメートル）を超え、宇宙へと向かった。

> 反意語を作る場合、接頭辞を変化させるものや、接頭辞を付加したり削除したりするものや、全く別の表現を使うものなどがあります。派生語はまとめて覚えるようにしましょう。

以下の1～7の語の反意語を [　　] 内に書き入れましょう。

1. ascend（上昇する）　　　　→ [　　　　　　　　　　　] （下降する）
2. ascent（上昇）　　　　　　→ [　　　　　　　　　　　] （下降）
3. attach（接続する）　　　　→ [　　　　　　　　　　　] （分離する）
4. attachment（接続）　　　　→ [　　　　　　　　　　　] （分離）
5. continue（続ける）　　　　→ [　　　　　　　　　　　] （中止する）
6. fix（取り付ける、固定する）→ [　　　　　　　　　　　] （取り外す）
7. launching（打ち上げ）　　　→ [　　　　　　　　　　　] （着陸）

時・条件・譲歩を表す接続詞節中では、〈主語＋be 動詞〉が省略されることがあります。以下の1と2の英文の（　　）内に当てはまる接続詞を選択肢から選び、書き入れましょう。ただし文頭に来る語も小文字で与えられています。

1. (　　　　　　　　　) detached, the capsule continues its trajectory several miles toward the sky.
   カプセルは、切り離されてから、上空に向かって数マイルも弾道飛行を続ける。

2. The descent is slowed down by a "feathering" system in which the spacecraft's tail pivots, (　　　　　　　) arching, (　　　　　　　) returning to normal and gliding to land.
   通常飛行に戻り滑空して着陸する前に、あたかも弧を描くように宇宙船の後尾が旋回する「フェザー」システムによって、下降スピードが落とされる。

before	after	as if

ヴァージン・ギャラクティック社とブルー・オリジン社が提供する宇宙旅行について、以下の英文に<u>述べられていない</u>ものを1〜4から選びましょう。

The passengers of Virgin Galactic and Blue Origin will not orbit the Earth, and the weightless experience will last just minutes. This is far different from the experience of the first-ever space tourists who paid tens of millions of dollars to travel to the International Space Station in the 2000s.

Having paid for a much cheaper ticket — costing $250,000 with Virgin Galactic, and $200,000 to $300,000 for Blue Origin, according to a Reuters report — the new round of space tourists will be propelled above the atmosphere before coming back down to Earth. By comparison, the ISS is in orbit 250 miles (400 kilometers) from our planet.

AFP-JIJI

1. 地球周回軌道には乗らない。
2. 数分の無重力体験ができる。
3. 国際宇宙ステーションに行く旅行よりは費用がかからない。
4. 地球から400キロメートルの高度にまで達する。

● Newspaper English

ニュース記事では情報を具体的にイメージしやすくするために、数字情報が挙げられることがよくあります。英語圏では mile（1マイル＝約1.6キロメートル）、foot（1フィート＝約30.48センチメートル）など、日本ではあまり馴染みのない単位もよく用いられますので、おおよその換算値を覚えておくとよいでしょう。

以下の1〜3の英文（　　）内の単位を表す表現を、必要があれば変化させて書き入れましょう。

1. "Space" begins at an altitude of 62 (mile → 　　　　　　).
「宇宙」は海抜62マイルから始まる。

2. The spaceship will be detached at around 49,000 (foot → 　　　　　　).
その宇宙船はおよそ49,000フィートのところで切り離されるだろう。

3. Six passengers take their place in a "capsule" fixed to the top of a 60-(foot → 　　　　　　)-long rocket.
6人の乗客は、全長60フィートのロケットの先端に取り付けられた「カプセル」の中の席に着く。

New era for space tourism: Flights from Virgin Galactic and Blue Origin could come in 2019

WASHINGTON — The two companies leading the pack in the pursuit of space tourism say they are just months away from their first out-of-this-world passenger flights — though neither has set a firm date.

Virgin Galactic, founded by British billionaire Richard 5 Branson, and Blue Origin, by Amazon creator Jeff Bezos, are racing to be the first to finish their tests, using radically different technology.

Their goal is to approach or pass through the imaginary line marking where space begins — either the Karman line, 10 at 100 kilometers (62 miles), or the 50-mile (80-km) boundary recognized by the U.S. Air Force. At this altitude, the sky looks dark and the curvature of the Earth can be seen clearly.

With Virgin Galactic, six passengers and two pilots are boarded onto SpaceShipTwo VSS Unity, which resembles a 15 private jet. The VSS Unity will be attached to a carrier spacecraft — the WhiteKnightTwo — from which it will be detached at around 49,000 feet (15,000 meters). Once released, the spaceship will fire up its rocket and head for the sky. 20

Then the passengers will float in zero gravity for several minutes before coming back to Earth.

The descent is slowed down by a "feathering" system in which the spacecraft's tail pivots, as if arching, before returning to normal and gliding to land at Virgin's 25 "spaceport" in the New Mexico desert. In total, the mission lasts between 90 minutes and two hours.

Blue Origin, meanwhile, has developed a system closer to the traditional rocket: the New Shepard.

On this journey, six passengers take their place in a 30 "capsule" fixed to the top of a 60-foot-long (18-meter) rocket. After launching, it is detached and continues its trajectory

out-of-this-world「奇想天外な」

firm「確定的な」

radically「根本的に」

curvature「湾曲」

carrier spacecraft「母船」

fire up...「〜に点火する」

float「浮かぶ」
zero gravity「無重力状態」

spaceport「宇宙船基地」
mission「宇宙飛行」
meanwhile「一方」

several miles toward the sky. During an April 29 test, the capsule made it to an altitude of 66 miles (106 kilometers).

After a few minutes of weightlessness, during which passengers can take in the view through large windows, the take in the view「景色をながめる」

5 capsule gradually falls back to Earth, with three large parachutes and retrorockets used to slow the spacecraft. retrorocket「逆噴射ロケット」

From take-off to landing, the flight took 10 minutes during the latest test. Until now, tests have only been carried out carry out...「〜を行う」

using dummies at Blue Origin's West Texas site. In June, Rob dummy「(人間の) 代用品」

10 Meyerson, one of its directors, said the first human tests would come "soon."

AFP-JIJI

● Summary

以下の空所 1 〜 4 に当てはまる語を選択肢から選び、書き入れましょう。

Two (¹·   ) companies are finalizing their plans to launch separate space tourism ventures. Each company uses different technology and the (²·   ) details differ in terms of expected altitude, duration and cost, but both companies are in the final testing stages. Though neither company has announced a specific date for their (³·   ) commercial flight, expectations are high that both will open for business in the (⁴·   ) months.

first	coming	competing	exact

以下の１と２のうちカーマン・ラインの説明をしているものを選びましょう。

1. An altitude of 100 kilometers above Earth's sea level is commonly considered the boundary between Earth's atmosphere and outer space.

2. The boundary lies at an altitude of 50 miles, where the sky is dark and the curved shaped of the Earth can be seen.

本文の内容に合うように、１と３の英文を完成させるのに適当なものを、２の質問の答えとして適当なものをａ～ｄから選びましょう。

1. Both companies behind the separate space tourism ventures
   a. use the same spacecraft to send different passenger capsules into space.
   b. are owned by business leaders.
   c. are offering various flights that peak at the same altitudes.
   d. are partially funded by the U.S. military budget.

2. What does the VSS Unity's "feathering" system allow it to do?
   a. Increase its ascent speed
   b. Decrease its ascent speed
   c. Increase its descent speed
   d. Decrease its descent speed

3. At the time of writing, Blue Origin had
   a. failed to exceed the Karman line.
   b. decided to use Virgin Galactic's "feathering" technology.
   c. yet to conduct a test flight with live passengers.
   d. just released the expected date for its first commercial flight.

Chapter 9

Save the World from Garbage!

世界のゴミに挑む！

The Yomiuri Shimbun

● Key Expressions 1　　　　　　　　　　　　◎ CD1-34

音声を聞いて1～3の（　　）内に適当な語を書き入れましょう。

1. The rapid economic development experienced across Southeast Asia has created a serious (g _ _ _ _ _ _) problem.
   東南アジア中で巻き起こっている急速な経済開発が、深刻なゴミ問題を生み出している。

2. The (a _ _ _ _ _) of waste has increased year by year.
   ゴミの量は年々増えている。

3. At most disposal sites across Southeast Asia, municipal solid waste is collected and (p _ _ _ _) up at a single site as an open dump.
   東南アジア中のほとんどのゴミ処理場では、都市固体廃棄物が集められ、戸外のゴミ捨て場として1か所に積み上げられている。

● Key Expressions 2

以下の1～6の語とほぼ同じ意味を表す語（句）を選択肢から選び、[　]内に書き入れましょう。

1. waste（ゴミ）　　　　　　　　[　　　　　　　　　]
2. accumulate（蓄積する）　　　　[　　　　　　　　　]
3. discard（捨てる）　　　　　　 [　　　　　　　　　]
4. incinerate（焼却する）　　　　 [　　　　　　　　　]
5. highlight（際立たせる）　　　　[　　　　　　　　　]
6. handle（対処する、取り扱う）　[　　　　　　　　　]

burn	dispose of	tackle	rubbish	emphasize	pile up

● Key Expressions 3

以下の1～4の英文の（　）内に当てはまる前置詞を選択肢から選び、書き入れましょう。複数回使うものもあります。また、文頭に来る語も小文字で与えられています。

1. (　　　　　　　　) a waste treatment site in Bantar Gebang, (　　　　　　　　) the suburbs of Jakarta, about 7,500 tons of garbage is collected and carried out (　　　　　　) the capital (　　　　　　) truck every day.
   ジャカルタ郊外のバンタルグバンのあるゴミ処理場では、毎日約7,500トンのゴミが集められ、首都からトラックで運び出される。

2. There will be no space here to discard garbage (　　　　　　) five years.
   5年後には、ここにはゴミを捨てるスペースはなくなるだろう。

3. Already (　　　　　　) Thailand, Chinese companies have received an increasing number of orders (　　　　　　) offering lower prices.
   もうすでにタイでは、中国企業が低価格を提供することで、ますます多くの注文を受けている。

4. Competition (　　　　　　) Japanese and Chinese companies is likely to intensify (　　　　　　) both quality and price.
   日本と中国の企業間の競争は、質と価格の両方を巡ってますます激しくなるだろう。

between	of	over	in	at	by

東南アジアのゴミ対策について、英文に述べられているものを 1 ～ 4 から選びましょう。

In Indonesia, President Joko Widodo announced in April 2018 that the country had made plans to build garbage incineration sites in 12 urban cities.

With support from the Japan International Cooperation Agency (JICA), a project is under way to build the country's first large-scale incineration facility in Legok Nangka, about 150 kilometers southeast of Jakarta. In recent years, the construction of garbage incineration sites has begun also in other countries such as Malaysia, the Philippines and Myanmar.

The Japan News

1. 日本はインドネシアの 12 都市にゴミの焼却所を建設する計画を立てている。

2. インドネシアは JICA の援助でジャカルタ南西部に大規模な焼却施設を建設予定である。

3. インドネシアは他の東南アジア諸国に先駆けてゴミ問題に取り組んできた。

4. マレーシア、フィリピン、ミャンマーでもゴミの焼却施設の建設が始まっている。

● **Newspaper English**

 時制には、記事を読む際の重要な情報が含まれています。現在時制は一般的な事実や不変の状態を述べる際に使われます。現在進行形は、今まさに進行中の事柄や近い未来に起こる事柄を、現在完了形は過去から今までに起こった事柄を表す場合に用いられます。

以下の 1 ～ 3 の英文の（　　）内の動詞を適当な時制に変えましょう。

1. In this problem (lie → 　　　　　　) an opportunity for Japanese companies with incineration expertise.
この問題の中には、ゴミ焼却が専門の日本企業にとってのチャンスが潜んでいる。

2. Japan, which (need → 　　　　　　) to dispose of a large amount of waste within its small territory, (develop → 　　　　　　) top-level technology and expertise in building incineration facilities.
日本は、小さな領土内で多量のゴミを処理する必要があるため、焼却施設建設においてトップレベルの技術と専門知識を発展させてきた。

3. Southeast Asia (attract → 　　　　　　) attention as a promising market.
東南アジアは前途有望な市場として注目を集めつつある。

S.E. = Southeast

Japanese firms see opportunity in S.E. Asia garbage

JAKARTA — The rapid economic development experienced across Southeast Asia has created a serious garbage problem, as growing volumes of rubbish highlight a shortage of disposal sites.

But in this problem lies an opportunity for Japanese 5 companies with incineration expertise to begin the urgent task of constructing badly needed disposal facilities.

At a waste treatment site in Bantar Gebang, in the suburbs of Jakarta, about 7,500 tons of garbage is collected and carried out of the capital by truck every day. The amount 10 of garbage at this site has increased year by year, accumulating on the 82-hectare plot into a pile that is 35 meters tall at the highest point, creating a mountain of garbage.

"In five years, there will be no space here to dispose of 15 garbage," a 35-year-old employee of the facility said with a sigh.

This situation is not limited to the Bantar Gebang site. At most disposal sites across Southeast Asia, municipal solid waste is collected and piled up at a single site as an open 20 dump. As economic development continues, every country in the region is finding the problem of garbage disposal increasingly difficult to tackle without incinerators.

Japan, which needs to dispose of a large amount of waste within its small territory, has developed top-level technology 25 and expertise in building incineration facilities.

State-of-the-art facilities built by Japanese companies, including Hitachi Zosen Corp. and JFE Engineering Corp., also generate power in the incineration process, which allows an early recovery of construction costs. In fact, about 30 30 percent of the existing incineration facilities in Japan — approximately 1,100 in total — are capable of generating power.

plot「区画」

incinerator「焼却炉」

state-of-the-art「最新の」

Japanese incinerator construction companies have increasingly found success in Europe and other regions, and Southeast Asia is attracting their attention as a promising market.

5   At the same time, there is an issue peculiar to emerging countries regarding the livelihoods of so-called waste pickers.

These manual laborers make their living by collecting and reselling recyclable materials such as plastic bottles and metals from open-dump disposal sites. About 10,000 people
10 are said to make a living this way around disposal sites in the suburbs of Jakarta, livelihoods that might disappear if that garbage was incinerated.

The Japan News

peculiar to... 「〜特有の」

emerging country 「新興国」

livelihood 「暮らし」

manual laborer 「肉体労働者」

make a living 「生計を立てる」

● **Summary**   ◎ CD1-37

以下の空所１〜４に当てはまる語を選択肢から選び、書き入れましょう。

Japanese incinerator construction companies are (¹·   ) to build on their expertise and enter (²·   ) markets across Southeast Asia. As garbage starts to pile up in open dumps around cities in countries like Indonesia, the technology developed by the companies might provide a possible answer, with the added benefit of (³·   ) electrical power through the incineration process. However, those who earn money through (⁴·   ) recyclable materials found in the waste might lose their livings if the waste is burned.

| generating | hoping | reselling | emerging |

本文の内容に合うものには T（True）を、合わないものには F（False）を（　）内に書き入れましょう。

1. Southeast Asia is a promising market for Japanese companies with incineration expertise. （　　）

2. At a waste treatment site in Bantar Gebang, there is a mountain of garbage more than 35 meters high. （　　）

3. In Southeast Asian countries, many incineration facilities have already been constructed. （　　）

4. Earning a living might become more difficult for waste pickers after the construction of incineration facilities. （　　）

本文の内容に合うように、1の質問の答えとして適当なものを、2と3の英文を完成させるのに適当なものを a 〜 d から選びましょう。

1. Why is the Bantar Gebang employee concerned?
   a. At the current rate, the site is likely to run out of space for the garbage.
   b. The mountain of waste is so high that it may collapse in the near future.
   c. The cost of buying more land and extending the facility is too high.
   d. The growing pile of garbage represents an environmental hazard.

2. The benefits of some Japanese incinerators include
   a. zero-emission energy production.
   b. very cheap construction costs.
   c. opportunities to generate revenues.
   d. 30 percent smaller incinerators.

3. One potential drawback of building incinerators in emerging countries noted in the article is that
   a. garbage truck drivers will eventually be forced to quit their jobs.
   b. fumes given off by burning plastic bottles could make people sick.
   c. it will be hard to find enough manual laborers to work on the site.
   d. incinerating garbage could deprive people of their source of income.

Chapter 10

Manga Featuring the Elderly

もう脇役ではありません

Kodansha (left) / Shinchosha (right)

● **Key Expressions 1**　　　　　　　　◎ CD1-38

音声を聞いて1～3の（　　）内に適当な語を書き入れましょう。

1. A new (g _ _ _ _) of manga with elderly main characters is increasing its presence as Japan's population rapidly ages.

日本の人口が急速に高齢化に向かうにつれ、高齢者が主役の新しいジャンルの漫画が存在感を増している。

2. Manga magazines have changed in (c _ _ _ _ _ _) along with the aging of generations who were acquainted with them in childhood.

子ども時代に漫画雑誌に親しんでいた世代の人たちの高齢化が進むにつれ、漫画雑誌の内容が変化してきた。

3. Featuring the elderly as leading characters, (r _ _ _ _ _) than in supporting roles, has shed light on details of what older people worry about and struggle with.

高齢者たちに、脇役ではなく主役を務めさせることで、高齢者が何を悩み、何と格闘しているかについての詳細を明らかにしている。

以下の 1 ～ 4 の賛否に関連する表現の（　　）内に当てはまる語を選択肢から選び、書き入れましょう。

1. be (　　　　　　　　)...　　　　　　　　［～に賛成する］
2. be (　　　　　　　　)...　　　　　　　　［～に反対する］
3. agree/disagree (　　　　　　　　)...　　　［～（人）に賛成 / 反対する］
4. (　　　　　　　) agreement/disagreement with...
　　　　　　　　　　　　　　　　　　　［～と意見が一致・不一致で］

| in | for | with | against |

現在完了形の〈have/has ＋過去分詞〉は、過去に起こったことと現在とのつながりを伝えるための表現です。

以下の 1 ～ 3 の英文は、2016 年に出版された女性向けコミック誌『ビーラブ』に掲載されたある漫画について説明をしている英文です。英文の下の情報を参考に、（　　）内に当てはまる動詞を選択肢から選び、適当な形に変化させて書き入れましょう。

1. She sets out from the home she (　　　　　　　　　　　) with her son.
   過去：この漫画の主人公の女性は以前息子と同居していた。
   現在：つい最近まで同居していて、今は家を出たばかり。

2. The manga (　　　　　　　　　　　) in *Be Love*, a manga for women published by Kodansha Ltd. since 2016.
   過去：2016 年に、『ビーラブ』にこの漫画が掲載された。
   現在：2016 年から今まで連載され続けている。

3. Kodansha (　　　　　　　　　　　) comments from many readers in their 40s and 50s who say the tale strikes a chord with them.
   過去：出版社は、この漫画に共感したという読者からのコメントを受けた。
   現在：そのようなコメントは今も届き続けている。

| serialize | receive | share |

お笑い芸人の矢部太郎氏が描いた漫画について、英文に述べられているものを 1 ～ 4 から選びましょう。

"Oya-san to Boku" ("The Landlady and Me") is a popular comic book in the genre, based on the life experiences of Taro Yabe, a 41-year-old comedian who lodges on the second floor of a house in Tokyo owned by a woman in her late 80s. The landlady divorced when she was young and lives alone in the house until Yabe moves in. The two develop a warm and friendly relationship. Yabe's story published by Shinchosha Publishing Co. has drawn a large following, with 410,000 copies in print. Many readers in their 30s and older write that they "yearn" for such a relationship.

Kyodo

1. 漫画は矢部氏の実体験に基づいている。
2. 漫画の主人公の大家さんは、所有する建物の 2 階に住んでいた。
3. 矢部氏の描いた漫画は、少ないが非常に熱心なファンがいる。
4. 30 歳代以上の読者は、漫画で描かれているような人間関係はあり得ないと感想を述べている。

● **Newspaper English**

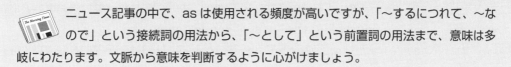

ニュース記事の中で、as は使用される頻度が高いですが、「～するにつれて、～なので」という接続詞の用法から、「～として」という前置詞の用法まで、意味は多岐にわたります。文脈から意味を判断するように心がけましょう。

以下の 1 ～ 3 に続く表現を a ～ c から選び、それぞれの as が接続詞もしくは前置詞のどちらであるかを答えましょう。

1. Mariko's new life begins (　　　).　　　　　　　　　　　　　　　［接続詞／前置詞］
2. The seventh volume is due to be released this month (　　　).［接続詞／前置詞］
3. Readers in their 40s and 50s imagine they themselves might experience similar situations (　　　).　　　　　　　　　　　　　　　［接続詞／前置詞］

   a. as an independent comic book
   b. as they get older
   c. as an internet cafe refugee

Manga starting to feature elderly characters

Japan is starting to embrace a new genre of manga featuring elderly people as the leading characters.

"Sanju Mariko" is a story about Mariko, a widow and writer who at the age of *sanju*, Japanese for 80, sets out from the home she has shared with her son, his wife and extended family, including her great-grandchild. Her new life begins as an "internet cafe refugee" after she is unable to secure other accommodations.

The decision to leave home is prompted by a feeling of alienation brought on by disagreements with her family over a plan to rebuild the house she had thought would be her final home, as well as a sense of loneliness after learning that a friend has died alone. She even ponders whether her family is hoping that she will die soon.

The story incorporates a variety of problems elderly people might encounter, such as driving the wrong way on a highway or turning their home into a "garbage dump" by hoarding items they consider treasures and do not want to part with.

Other themes in the work include love affairs among the elderly and the onset of senile dementia.

"Sanju Mariko" has been serialized since 2016 in *Be Love*, a manga for women published by Kodansha Ltd. As an independent comic book, the seventh volume is due to be released this month.

Kodansha has received comments from many readers in their 40s and 50s who say the tale strikes a chord with them because they imagine they themselves might experience similar situations as they get older.

But while Mariko worries about her situation, she also stays positive and actively faces new challenges as she forms relationships with others.

The author of "Sanju Mariko," Yuki Ozawa, 53, empathizes

embrace...「〜を受け入れる」

extended family「拡大家族」

refugee「難民」
accommodation「宿泊する場所」
prompt...「〜を促す」
alienation「疎外感」

ponder...「〜を考える」

incorporate...「〜を取り入れる」

hoard...「〜をため込む」

onset「始まり」
senile dementia「老人性認知症」
be due to...「〜することになっている」

empathize with...「〜に共感する」

with the anxiety about the future felt by people of her generation. But she says "there are more elderly people who frequent gaming arcades, and it seems people of my generation, who experienced the bubble economy when they
5 were young, still have the curiosity of youth."

frequent... 「〜に足繁く通う」

curiosity 「好奇心」

"Mariko, in a sense, is my ideal and I feel as if there will be more elderly like her," Ozawa said.

This new genre of manga stories allows readers to identify with such characters and think about social problems they
10 themselves will face in old age while considering the ideal role model for the elderly, experts say.

identify with... 「〜と重ね合わせる」

Kyodo

● **Summary** CD1-41

以下の空所1〜4に当てはまる語句を選択肢から選び、書き入れましょう。

A number of new manga series featuring elderly protagonists have led observers to note the emergence of a new genre within the artform of manga. These series (1.   ) the creators and readers to (2.   ) many of the issues faced by Japan's elderly population. These issues (3.   ) feelings of isolation, romantic relationships and coping with illness. Many fans of the genre are middle-aged people who are starting to (4.   ) to their old age and think about new ideals for later life.

| include | explore | look ahead | allow |

本文に紹介されている漫画の主人公「傘寿まり子」について、以下の英文の（　　）内に当てはまる抽象名詞を選択肢からすべて選び○で囲みましょう。

A sense of (　　　　　　　　　) prompts Mariko's decision to leave home where she has lived with her son's family.

togetherness	loneliness	urgency	alienation	remorse

本文の内容に合うように、1と3の英文を完成させるのに適当なものを、2の質問の答えとして適当なものをa〜dから選びましょう。

1. Mariko is a woman who
   a. decides to divorce her husband at the age of 80.
   b. moves in with her old friend to avoid loneliness.
   c. experiences conflict with her family regarding their house.
   d. opens an internet cafe to keep herself busy.

2. Which of the following is NOT mentioned as a theme in "Sanju Mariko"?
   a. Romantic relationships between older people
   b. Injuries caused by physical frailty
   c. Driving in the wrong direction on a freeway
   d. Holding on to objects with personal significance

3. Yuki Ozawa believes that
   a. elderly people should read more and spend less time in gaming arcades.
   b. the inspiration for Mariko came from her observations of her own mother.
   c. the number of readers who might identify with Mariko will increase.
   d. living through Japan's bubble economy has damaged her generation.

Chapter 11

Why Not Go to Kyoto?
採用戦線は京都にあり

The Yomiuri Shimbun

● Key Expressions 1

音声を聞いて1〜3の（　　）内に適当な語を書き入れましょう。

1. More and more IT companies, which are based in other prefectures, have been (l _ _ _ _ _ _ _ _) offices in the heart of the city of Kyoto.

他の都道府県に本拠がある IT 企業で、京都市中心部にオフィスを開設するところがますます増加している。

2. Firms in the information technology sector are facing fierce (c _ _ _ _ _ _ _ _ _ _) in their recruiting due to a growing demand for IT engineers.

IT 業界の企業は、IT 技術者に対する需要の高まりのため、採用活動で熾烈な競争に直面している。

3. Many companies aim to (s _ _ _ _ _) capable human resources by taking advantage of the attractive features of the ancient capital.

多くの企業は、古都の魅力的特徴を利用することによって、能力のある人材を確保することを目指している。

● Key Expressions 2

以下の1～6の就職や採用活動に関係する日本語の意味になるように、（　　）内に当てはまる語を選択肢から選び、書き入れましょう。

1. 求人　　　　　　job（　　　　　　　　　　）
2. 求職申込　　　　job（　　　　　　　　　　）
3. 転職　　　　　　job（　　　　　　　　　　）
4. 採用基準　　　　recruitment（　　　　　　　　　）
5. 人材派遣会社　　recruitment（　　　　　　　　　）
6. 採用活動　　　　recruitment（　　　　　　　　　）

| agency | standards | application | change | drive | opening |

● Key Expressions 3

英語には、同じスペリングで名詞と動詞の両方の意味・機能を持つ語が数多くあります。

（例）	名詞	動詞
gear	歯車、装置・装備	向ける、対象とする
staff	職員、スタッフ	配属する
headquarter	（しばしば複数形で）本社、本部	本社を置く

以下の1～3の英文の（　　）内に当てはまる語を上記の枠内から選び、必要なら形を変えて書き入れましょう。

1. Many companies (　　　　　　　　　　　) in places other than Kyoto Prefecture have been opening development bases in the heart of the ancient capital city.

2. The office is currently (　　　　　　　　　　　) by about 10 regular workers.

3. "We don't have any preferential tax incentives or other benefits (　　　　　　　　　　) toward IT companies," said an official.

最近の IT 業界の就職環境や企業の採用活動について、英文に<u>述べられていないもの</u>を 1 ～ 4 から選びましょう。

The Tokyo metropolitan area is suffering shortages of engineers in artificial intelligence and other IT fields. The ratio of job openings to job applicants in the IT field hit 4.06 in Tokyo in October 2018, but the ratio stood at 1.9 in Kyoto, meaning it is comparatively easier for companies to find IT engineers in the old capital.

"The work styles have diversified," said Kaoru Fujii, editor-in-chief at Rikunabi Next, a service for mid-career job seekers. "If companies hire at their own convenience only, employees will not stay long."

The Japan News

1. IT 業界における求人倍率は、2018 年 10 月時点で東京では 4.06 倍、京都で 1.9 倍だった。
2. IT 企業への就職希望者は東京よりも京都の方が多い。
3. リクナビ NEXT の藤井編集長によると、仕事のスタイルが多様化してきている。
4. 自社の都合だけで雇用する企業には従業員は居つかないと、藤井氏は述べた。

● Newspaper English

助動詞 can/may/will の過去形 could/might/would には仮定法の用法があります。仮定法として使用した場合は、筆者・話者が「断定を避けている」、あるいは「より可能性が低いと考えている」ことが示唆されます。ただし、その違いを日本語で明確に訳し分けることは難しい場合もあります。

助動詞の形に注意して、以下の 1 と 2 の英文の日本語訳を完成させましょう。

1. There are increasing concerns among companies that a labor shortage could blunt their growth.
   労働者不足が＿＿＿＿＿＿＿＿＿＿＿＿＿＿＿＿＿＿＿＿＿という懸念が、
   企業の中で増大している。

2. More IT companies have thought that launching branches in Kyoto would be more beneficial with respect to their recruitment.
   求人という点で、京都に支店を開設することが＿＿＿＿＿＿＿＿＿＿＿＿＿
   ＿＿＿＿＿＿と考える企業が増えてきている。

Kyoto popular spot for IT firms, branches

KYOTO — An increasing number of companies based outside Kyoto Prefecture have been setting up offices in the central part of Kyoto, as part of their efforts to secure capable human resources by taking advantage of the city's name recognition. 5

Kyoto is not just famous at home and abroad, it is also home to many universities. Many companies headquartered in places other than Kyoto Prefecture — mostly those in the information technology sector — have been opening design offices or development bases in the heart of the ancient 10 capital city with the aim of making their recruitment drives easier amid increasing concerns that a labor shortage could blunt their growth.

In October 2018, Fenrir Inc., an Osaka-based startup developing smartphone apps, set up its Kyoto branch office in 15 a building near Shijo-Karasuma, one of the main crossings in the center of the city. The 210-square-meter office is currently staffed by about 10 regular workers but can accommodate up to about 30 staff members.

The biggest feature of the office is set to be a section called 20 the "Project Room," which is scheduled to open this spring and will account for half of the entire floor space. The room is designed to facilitate joint development with universities and interactions with students and other companies.

Keiichi Totsuka, head of the branch office, said his 25 company aims to make the room "a place where students can gain up-to-date information," thus promoting its edge and ultimately making it easier to find capable human resources.

In the same neighborhood as Fenrir's new office, LINE Corp., a major Tokyo-based communications app operator, 30 also opened its development base in June 2018. Another Tokyo firm, Money Forward, Inc., opened its development base near the city's Sanjo-Kawaramachi crossing in February

name recognition「知名度」

be home to...「〜の所在地である」

design office「設計事務所」
development base「開発拠点」

Fenrir Inc.「フェンリル株式会社」
startup「新興企業」
main crossing「主要交差点」
accommodate ...「〜を収容する」
be set to...「〜することになっている」
account for...「〜を占める」
facilitate...「〜を促進する」
joint development「共同開発」

up-to-date「最新の」
edge「競争力」
LINE Corp.「LINE 株式会社」
operator「業者」

Money Forward, Inc.「株式会社マネーフォワード」

2019.

"We don't have any preferential tax incentives or other benefits geared toward IT companies," said an official of the Kyoto municipal government in charge of encouraging companies to operate businesses in the city.

5 Even so, more and more companies have set up offices in central Kyoto because they are facing fierce competition in their recruitment drives. "There are many job seekers who are interested in living and working in Kyoto. This is true for both new graduates and mid-career job candidates," a Money 10 Forward spokesperson said.

The Japan News

preferential tax incentive
「税制上の優遇措置」
benefit「支援」
the Kyoto municipal
government「京都市役所」

mid-career job candidate「中
途採用希望者」

● **Summary**   CD2-05

以下の空所1～4に当てはまる語を選択肢から選び、書き入れましょう。

A number of IT companies are opening up offices in Kyoto in a bid to attract the kinds of (¹·   ) workers that are in (²·   ) supply in metropolitan areas like Tokyo and Osaka. Living and working in the (³·   ) capital city has its appeal, so companies have decided it is easier to be where the talent wants to be, rather than trying to lure them to the (⁴·   ) cities in which the companies' headquarters are located.

| skilled | large | ancient | short |

以下の１〜３の英文の（　　）内に当てはまる企業名を選択肢から選び、書き入れましょう。

1. (   ) launched a development base near Shijo-Karasuma in June 2018.

2. A spokesperson of (   ) suggested that Kyoto is appealing to people at various career stages.

3. (   ) is willing to collaborate with universities not only to co-develop new apps but to employ capable graduates.

| Fenrir   LINE   Money Forward |

本文の内容に合うように、１の質問の答えとして適当なものを、２と３の英文を完成させるのに適当なものをａ〜ｄから選びましょう。

1. Which of the following aspects of Kyoto is NOT discussed in the article as part of its appeal?

   a. Its name is well-known both domestically and overseas.

   b. Many institutions of higher education are located there.

   c. Some firms are finding it easier to find suitable workers there.

   d. The startup costs for IT firms are lower there.

2. The Kyoto branch of Fenrir Inc.

   a. is situated just on the outskirts of the city.

   b. contains a 210 m^2 "Project Room."

   c. is currently staffed by 10 university students.

   d. has space for an additional 20 employees.

3. The boom in Kyoto satellite offices is despite the fact that

   a. many Tokyo-based employees do not wish to move there.

   b. the city is already saturated with new branches of tech firms.

   c. the local government offers no particular financial incentives aimed at the IT sector.

   d. the local government wants to preserve the city's traditional image.

Chapter 12

To Be More Eco-friendly

ラグジュアリーブランドの環境戦略

EPA/JIJI

● **Key Expressions 1**　　　　　　　　　　　　　　◎ CD2-06

音声を聞いて1～3の（　　）内に適当な語を書き入れましょう。

1. The United Nations warned that the fashion (i _ _ _ _ _ _ _) needs a course correction.

国際連合は、ファッション産業は軌道修正が必要であると警告を発した。

2. An up-and-coming brand created a new dress out of unsold clothing and other (m _ _ _ _ _ _ _).

ある新進ブランドは、売れ残った衣類と他の素材から新しいドレスを作り上げた。

3. Upcycling is a method of changing discarded products into items with high added (v _ _ _ _).

アップサイクルとは、廃棄された製品を高い付加価値を持つ商品に作り替える手法のことである。

以下は企業の組織に関する語句です。日本語の意味になるように、1 〜 5 の（　　）内に当てはまる語句を選択肢から選び、書き入れましょう。

1. 広報課 　　　　　（　　　　　　　　　　　　　） Division

2. 人事部 　　　　　（　　　　　　　　　　　　　） Department

3. 研究開発課 　　　（　　　　　　　　　　　　　） Division

4. 経理課 　　　　　（　　　　　　　　　　　　　） Division

5. 法務部 　　　　　（　　　　　　　　　　　　　） Department

Accounting	Legal	Public Relations
Personnel	Research and Development	

日本語訳を参考に、以下の 1 〜 3 の英文の（　　）内に当てはまる語を選択肢から選び、書き入れましょう。

1. Animal rights organizations in about 30 countries criticized Prada by
（　　　　　　）.
およそ 30 か国の動物愛護団体が、プラダを名指しで批判した。

2. A select shop company carefully crafts one-of-a-kind items by (　　　　　　).
あるセレクトショップ会社は、独自の商品を丁寧に手作業で作り上げる。

3. The substance was discovered by (　　　　　　).
その物質は偶然発見された。

---

hand	chance	name

株式会社岡田織物について、英文に<u>述べられていないもの</u>を1～4から選びましょう。

　Okada Textile Co. in Hashimoto, Wakayama Prefecture, uses acrylic materials developed by Mitsubishi Chemical Corp. to manufacture fake fur that recreates the color, luster and even feel of real fur. After Gucci's announcement last year that it would no longer use fur, Okada Textile has received continuing inquiries from both domestic and international brands. The company president said, "Inquiries have doubled compared to this time last year." Visitors to their sales website once only numbered about 100 a day, but now there are days when the number of visitors surges to 1,000.

The Japan News

Notes　acrylic「アクリルの」　luster「光沢」

1. 三菱ケミカル株式会社が開発したアクリル素材を使用している。
2. 岡田織物のフェイク・ファーは、本物の毛皮の色や光沢だけでなく手触りまで再現している。
3. 去年の今頃と比べて、製品に関する問い合わせの数が10倍になった。
4. 同社の販売サイトの訪問者数は、今や日に1,000人になることもある。

● **Newspaper English**

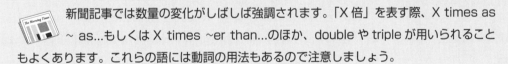
新聞記事では数量の変化がしばしば強調されます。「X倍」を表す際、X times as ~ as...もしくはX times ~er than...のほか、double や triple が用いられることもよくあります。これらの語には動詞の用法もあるので注意しましょう。

日本語訳を参考に、以下の1～3の英文の（　　）内の語のうち適当なものを○で囲みましょう。

1. The population has become (three times / triple) larger than ten years ago.
　 人口は10年前の3倍になった。

2. Sales have (doubled / twiced) over the last three years.
　 過去3年間で売上が2倍になった。

3. The figure is (double more / double) the number during the economic bubble.
　 その数字はバブル経済期の数の2倍である。

sustainable「持続可能な」

account for...「～を占める」

carbon dioxide emissions
「二酸化炭素排出量」

Ellen MacArthur Foundation
「エレン・マッカーサー財団」
fall short of...「～に届かない」

Fur Free Alliance「ファーフ
リーアライアンス（毛皮に反対
する国際団体）」
animal rights organization
「動物権利団体、動物愛護団体」
clarify...「～を明らかにする」

mass production and
disposal「大量生産と大量廃
棄」

inventory「在庫」

circulate「流通する」
Economy, Trade and
Industry Ministry「経済産業
省」

Can the fashion industry become more sustainable?

In March 2018, the United Nations held an international event in Switzerland on the topic of fashion and sustainable development goals. The fashion industry uses the second-largest volume of water among all industries, and accounts for 20 percent of the world's wastewater and 10 percent of 5 global carbon dioxide emissions. The United Nations warned that the industry needs a course correction.

A research report concerning clothing issued in November 2017 by the Britain-based Ellen MacArthur Foundation also pointed out that the recycling rate for clothing falls short of 10 even 1 percent.

The use of fur receives criticism, too. In September 2018, during Prada's show in Milan, not a single piece of clothing used fur. Shortly before the show, the Fur Free Alliance, representing animal rights organizations from about 30 15 countries, released a statement criticizing Prada by name. This spread on social networking services and Prada received thousands of protest emails and phone calls, according to Prada's public relations division. Prada further clarified that it would gradually scale down the use of fur in its products. 20

The movement to take another look at mass production and disposal has also begun to expand in Japan. In October 2017, the select shop Beams Co. started its brand Beams Couture that recycles some of the clothing and materials sitting in its inventory. 25

According to Beams' public relations division, "It is a challenge to change clothing sleeping in the warehouse into unique pieces with value through the power of design."

There are about 4 billion pieces of clothing circulating in Japan, according to a 2016 Economy, Trade and Industry 30 Ministry survey. This figure is double the number during the economic bubble. The volume of textile garbage, including discarded clothing, increased to about 1.21 million tons, according to a fiscal 2015 Environment Ministry survey.

Professor Yoshinori Terui of Bunka Fashion Graduate University said, "It is time to consider a framework that uses tools such as artificial intelligence to create clothing without the need for large amounts of stock. Consumers must focus their attention more on the production process on the other side of beautiful clothing."

Environment Ministry「環境省」

production process「生産過程」

The Japan News

● **Summary** CD2-09

以下の空所 1 〜 4 に当てはまる語を選択肢から選び、書き入れましょう。

The fashion industry is (1.   ) under increasing scrutiny in terms of its environmental impact. Observers note that clothing manufacturers both use up large amounts of natural resources and contribute to global waste products. In response, businesses and educators are (2.   ) into ways to improve sustainability, including (3.   ) unused materials and (4.   ) advantage of artificial intelligence to minimize the necessary resources.

looking	coming	upcycling	taking

以下の1〜4の出来事を、実際に起こった順序に並べかえましょう。

1. An alliance of animal rights organizations criticized Prada for using fur.
2. The select shop Beams Co. started the Beams Couture brand.
3. The United Nations issued a warning to the fashion industry, saying that it needed a course correction.
4. A research report pointed out that the recycling rate for clothing falls short of even one percent.

(   ) → (   ) → (   ) → (   )

本文の内容に合うように、1〜3の英文を完成させるのに適当なものをa〜dから選びましょう。

1. According to the article, the fashion industry
   a. is surpassed by only one other industry in terms of water consumption.
   b. uses up 20 percent of the wastewater produced by other industries.
   c. is the second-largest producer of CO_2 emissions in the world.
   d. released a statement correcting the United Nations.

2. In response to the statement from the Fur Free Alliance, Prada
   a. immediately and permanently ceased production of all fur products.
   b. promised to reduce its use of fur to less than one percent.
   c. postponed the Milan show for its all-fur collection until September 2018.
   d. confirmed that it was working to reduce the use of fur in its collections.

3. Prof. Yoshinori Terui thinks it will be important to
   a. increase the number of consumers investing in artificial intelligence.
   b. return to more handcrafted garments and avoid the use of technology.
   c. raise the level of consumer awareness regarding clothing production.
   d. develop artificial intelligence that can create beautiful clothes.

Chapter 13

A Pleasant Night's Sleep at a Capsule Hotel

カプセルホテルで快適な眠りを

The Yomiuri Shimbun

● Key Expressions 1

CD2-10

音声を聞いて1～3の（　　）内に適当な語を書き入れましょう。

1. The history of capsule hotels may be one reason for their (p _ _ _ _ _ _ _ _).
カプセルホテルの歴史が、その人気の理由の一つだろう。

2. The first capsule hotel, which (p _ _ _ _ _ _ _) ultra-small guest rooms about the size of a single bed, opened in Osaka 40 years ago.
シングルベッドとほぼ同じ大きさの超小型客室を提供した最初のカプセルホテルは、40年前に大阪で開業した。

3. Foreign tourists also like the uniqueness of capsule hotels, and the number of these hotels is on the increase (o _ _ _ _ _ _ _).
外国人観光客もカプセルホテルの独自性を好んでおり、その数は海外で増えつつある。

-th は、性質や状態などを表す形容詞に付いて名詞を形成する接尾辞です。スペルがかなり変化するものもありますから、注意しましょう。

枠内の説明を参考に、以下の 1 〜 5 の形容詞を -th を含む名詞にしましょう。

1. wide（幅広い）　　　　　　　→[　　　　　　　　　]（幅、幅広さ）

2. deep（深い、奥行きが深い）　→[　　　　　　　　　]（深さ、奥行き）

3. long（長い）　　　　　　　　→[　　　　　　　　　]（長さ）

4. strong（強い）　　　　　　　→[　　　　　　　　　]（強さ、強度）

5. true（真実の）　　　　　　　→[　　　　　　　　　]（真実）

日本語訳を参考に、以下の 1 〜 4 の英文の ［　　］ 内の語句を並べかえましょう。

1. It [be / to / difficult / would] increase the number of hotels immediately in Japan.
即座に日本国内のホテル数を増やすのは難しいだろう。

_____

2. It was easy [quickly / to / capsule hotels / open] on small sites or in existing buildings.
狭い敷地や既存のビル内に素早くカプセルホテルを開業するのは容易だった。

_____

3. It was attractive [companies / to / open / for] capsule hotels because the legal requirements were less strict than those for ordinary hotels.
普通のホテルほど法的要件が厳しくないため、企業にとってはカプセルホテルを開業することは魅力的だった。

_____

4. It is necessary [to / companies / for / meet] the requirements of the building regulations.
企業は建築基準の要件を満たす必要がある。

_____

人気の２つのカプセルホテルの特徴について、英文に<u>述べられていないもの</u>を１～４から選びましょう。

Nine Hours, operated by a hotel chain, is popular among women, with its first capsule hotel opening in Kyoto in 2009. It is separated by gender, and has earned a reputation as being clean and neat. People can also use its showers without having to stay the night.

Meanwhile, First Cabin Inc. started a service reminiscent of an aircraft's first-class seats, opening its first hotel in Osaka's busy Nanba district in 2009. It now runs more than 20 capsule hotels.

The Japan News

1. ナインアワーズは開業当時、京都では初めてのカプセルホテルであった。

2. ナインアワーズでは宿泊客でなくても、ホテルのシャワーを使用することができる。

3. ファーストキャビンは、飛行機のファーストクラスを彷彿とさせるサービスを始めた。

4. ファーストキャビンは 2009 年に 1 号店を開業し、現在では 20 を超えるカプセルホテルを経営している。

● Newspaper English

英字新聞では「多くの」を表す際、many や a lot of 以外に a large number of や a large amount of といった表現も頻繁に用いられます。後に続く名詞が可算名詞の場合は number を、不可算名詞の場合には amount を使いましょう。

以下の１～３の英文の（　　）内に、number か amount のどちらかを書き入れましょう。

1. The legal requirements were less strict than those for ordinary hotels, and capsule hotels did not need a large (　　　　　　　) of space.
法的要件が普通のホテルほど厳しくなく、カプセルホテルは広いスペースも必要としなかった。

2. Kyoto receives a large (　　　　　　　) of tourists from all across the globe.
世界中から多くの観光客が京都を訪れる。

3. The company spent a large (　　　　　　　) of money on building a new luxury hotel.
その企業は新しい豪華ホテルの建設に大金を費やした。

The secrets of capsule hotels popularity

New Japan Co. 「ニュージャパン観光株式会社」

house... 「～を収容する、持つ」

prosper 「(経済的に) 繁栄する、成長する」

accommodation 「宿泊施設」

dimly lit 「薄暗い」

corridors 「通路」

lure... away from ~ 「…を (誘い出して) ～から乗り換えさせる」

mark a turning point 「転換点となる」

Labor Standards Law 「労働基準法」

In a busy quarter of Kita Ward, Osaka, New Japan Co. opened Capsule Inn Osaka in 1979 in a building that housed a 24-hour sauna facility.

At that time, Osaka was prospering and the rest area of the sauna was always packed with workers who had been 5 drinking, so the company decided to provide accommodation and open a hotel in the building. "We wanted to provide them with a pleasant night's sleep," a New Japan spokesman said.

The office of architect Kisho Kurokawa (1934-2007) designed the hotel. About 400 capsules — each measuring 90 10 centimeters in width and height and 1.9 meters long — lined both sides of dimly lit corridors in a two-story arrangement. The futuristic capsule design drew a lot of attention, and the hotel was always crowded with people, including those who had missed their last train home. 15

Before long, other companies opened capsule hotels, mainly in the urban centers of Tokyo and Osaka. It was attractive for companies to open capsule hotels because the legal requirements were less strict than those for ordinary hotels, and they did not need a large amount of space. This 20 meant it was easy to open them quickly on small sites or in existing buildings.

The bubble economy's burst in the early 1990s, however, changed the situation. In order to reduce costs, companies cut overtime and budgets for entertaining clients. Internet 25 cafes and manga-library coffee shops, which both allow people to sleep at more reasonable prices, lured customers away from capsule hotels.

But women's increased participation in the workforce marked a turning point — the revised Labor Standards Law 30 and revised Equal Employment Opportunity Law that went into force in 1999 increased female users. Stylish capsule hotels for women opened one after another, and the reputation of capsule hotels as being just a place for middle-aged men changed.

Recently, capsule hotels have started to open in foreign countries, mainly in Asia — at Incheon Airport in South Korea, a capsule hotel opened in 2017 for passengers of midnight flights. A foreign research company estimates that the world market size will be about ¥25 billion by the end of 2022.

The Japan News

Equal Employment Opportunity Law「男女雇用機会均等法」

go into force「(法律などが) 施行される」

● Summary

以下の空所 1 ～ 4 に当てはまる語を選択肢から選び、書き入れましょう。

Since their creation around 40 years ago, capsule hotels have continued to evolve and find (1.   ) clients and markets. The (2.   ) sleeping capsules were initially popular among male workers looking for somewhere to stay after (3.   ) nights spent socializing during Japan's bubble economy. The hotels were appealing to owners as they were quick and easy to set up. Over time, the popularity of capsule hotels has spread among the (4.   ) number of women in the Japanese workforce, and they have even been opened abroad.

growing	small	new	late

以下の 1 ～ 4 の出来事を、実際に起こった順序に並べかえましょう。

1. A new capsule hotel opened at an international airport in South Korea.
2. The revised Equal Employment Opportunity Law went into force.
3. Internet cafes and manga-library coffee shops lured customers away from capsule hotels.
4. The bubble economy ended.

    (   ) → (   ) → (   ) → (   )

本文の内容に合うように、1 ～ 3 の英文を完成させるのに適当なものを a ～ d から選びましょう。

1. New Japan Co. decided to open Capsule Inn Osaka because
   a. there was no money to be made in the 24-hour sauna business.
   b. they were asked to do so by their customers.
   c. capsule hotels were becoming popular in rural areas.
   d. there was nowhere for business men to get a pleasant night's sleep after socializing until late.

2. Capsule hotels were attractive business propositions because
   a. the government offered legal subsidies to hotel owners.
   b. they could be opened in existing buildings not originally intended for hotels.
   c. they could enforce stricter rules on customers staying there.
   d. many ordinary hotels were closing due to high running costs.

3. From 1999, the number of women staying in capsule hotels increased because
   a. laws forbidding them from using the hotels were abolished.
   b. many women also became hotel owners around the same time.
   c. they were attracted to the retro design of the older capsule hotels.
   d. new laws meant the number of working women began to increase.

Chapter 14

Healthy Lifestyles Discount Premium

健康志向社会が保険を変える

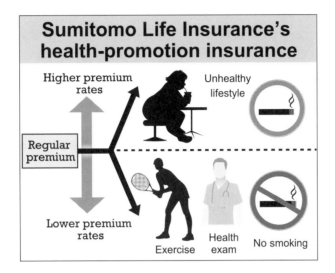

Sumitomo Life Insurance's health-promotion insurance

Higher premium rates — Unhealthy lifestyle

Regular premium

Lower premium rates — Exercise — Health exam — No smoking

● Key Expressions 1

 CD2-14

音声を聞いて 1 〜 3 の（　　）内に適当な語を書き入れましょう。

1. Life insurers are offering (d _ _ _ _ _ _ _ _) premiums to customers who improve their health or lifestyle, such as by exercising more or quitting smoking.

   生命保険各社が、運動量を増やしたり禁煙したりして健康状態やライフスタイルを改善する顧客には割引保険料を提供している。

2. If the insurers can encourage customers to pay more attention to (m _ _ _ _ _ _ _) their health, the incidence of disease could fall, leading to fewer insurance payouts.

   保険各社が顧客に健康管理にもっと注意を払うように仕向けることができれば、病気の発症率が下がり、保険金の支払いが少なくなるかもしれない。

3. With conventional insurance products, premiums are determined based on sex and age, and customers in the same (c _ _ _ _ _ _ _) are charged the same rate.

   従来の保険商品は、保険料は性別や年齢に基づいて決まり、同じ部類の顧客には一律の保険料が科される。

複数の意味を持つ単語の意味を特定するときは、記事の文脈をしっかり捉えることが必要です。

日本語訳を参考に、以下の1～3のそれぞれの英文の（　）内に共通して当てはまる語を書き入れましょう。

1. ・take (　　　　　　　) to improve one's health [自身の健康増進のために対策を講じる]

　　・people who make it a rule to walk an average of 8,000 (　　　　　　　) per day [一日に平均8000歩歩くことにしている人たち]

2. ・Healthier lifestyles will (　　　　　　) off. [より健康なライフスタイルは報われる]

　　・Customers have to (　　　　　　) extra amounts for the special feature.

　　　　　　　　　　　　　[顧客は、その特約分として余分に支払わねばならない]

3. ・He is three years (　　　　　　　) to me. [彼は私より3歳年上だ]

　　・He is a (　　　　　　) executive at the life insurance company.

　　　　　　　　　　　　　　　[彼はその生命保険会社の幹部役員である]

比較級の文では通常 than を用いますが、比較の対象が明らかな場合や、漠然と程度の違いを表す場合などは、than...を伴わないこともあります。

以下の1～3の英文の（　）内に当てはまる形容詞を選択肢から選び、比較級に変化させて書き入れましょう。ただし、文頭に来る語も小文字で与えられています。

1. With people having (　　　　　　　) children and getting married (　　　　　　　) in life, the life insurance industry is struggling to find new policyholders.

少子化や晩婚化につれ、生命保険業界は生命保険の新規加入者を見つけるのに苦戦している。

2. Customers will receive (　　　　　　　) discounts if certain conditions are met.

顧客は、特定の条件に当てはまれば、さらなる割引を受けるだろう。

3. (　　　　　　　) analyses of the data are needed to determine the refund amounts.

払戻金の額を決定するのに、さらに綿密なデータ分析が必要である。

deep	late	few	large

生命保険加入について、以下の英文に<u>述べられていないもの</u>を1〜4から選びましょう。

Since many people do not start thinking about life insurance until they get married or have a child, the growing tendency to marry later in life has slowed the influx of new customers. According to the Life Insurance Association of Japan, the number of new individual insurance contracts in fiscal 2017 was down about 10 percent from the previous year, to 17.27 million. However, with people living longer, there is more awareness of the importance of extending one's years of good health, which might raise the number of new customers.

The Japan News

1. 結婚や出産を契機に加入を考える人が多い。

2. 結婚を契機に新規加入する人が近年増加している。

3. 生命保険協会によると、2017年度の新規加入者の数は前年度より1割程度減った。

4. 健康に対する意識の高まりが新規加入者数の増加につながる可能性がある。

● **Newspaper English**

 ニュース記事に添えられているグラフや表は記事内容をサポートする重要な情報です。記事を読む前に内容を把握しておくと、記事理解が深まります。

以下の健康増進型の保険商品の表を参照して、1と2の保険商品を提供している保険会社の名前を下の選択肢a〜dから選びましょう。

Main health-promotion insurance products

Company	Product	Details
Sumitomo Life Insurance	*Vitality*	Premiums for next year lowered based on health exam, amount of exercise, other factors.
Tokio Marine & Nichido Life Insurance	*Aruku Hoken*	Premiums partially refunded for walking at least 8,000 steps per day on average.
Dai-ichi Life Insurance	*Kenshin-wari*	Premiums discounted for submitting health exam results when purchasing the product.
Sompo Japan Nipponkoa Himawari Life Insurance	*Jibun to Kazoku no Omamori*	Premiums discounted based on health and lifestyle improvements, such as lowering blood pressure and quitting smoking.

Vitality and *Kenshin-wari* are special contracts.

1. 運動することで、保険料の一部が払い戻される。［　　　　］

2. 加入時に健康診断書を提出すると保険料が割り引かれる。［　　　　］

a. 住友生命保険	**b.** 東京海上日動あんしん生命
c. 第一生命保険	**d.** 損保ジャパン日本興亜ひまわり生命

Insurers reward healthy lifestyles

reward... 「～に見返りを与える」

With people having fewer children and getting married later in life, the life insurance industry is struggling to find new policyholders. They hope that focusing on the buzzword "health" will open the door to a new source of customers.

buzzword 「うたい文句」

debut... 「～を売り出す」

Sumitomo Life Insurance Co. plans to debut its new 5 Vitality product on Tuesday, offering discounted premiums to customers who take steps to improve their health, such as by exercising more or changing their diet.

special feature 「特約」
enrollee 「加入者」

Sumitomo plans to include this special feature in its life, medical and other insurance plans. Enrollees will receive a 10 15 percent discount on monthly premiums simply by joining its program. Customers can then earn points for getting health exams, taking a certain number of steps each day and other achievements.

achievement 「成果」

up to... 「最大～まで」
in contrast 「逆に」

Those who earn enough points will receive further 15 discounts of up to 30 percent. In contrast, earning only a small number of points will actually lead to a premium increase of up to 10 percent.

This special feature will cost an extra ¥864 per month. If customer health improves and the incidence of disease 20 declines, the amount insurers pay out for medical insurance and other fees will also decrease.

decline 「減る、下がる」
fee 「料金（ここでは保険金）」

Other firms are offering similar products in an effort to create demand. Last August, Tokio Marine & Nichido Life Insurance Co. began offering Aruku Hoken, a medical 25 insurance product that offers partial refunds to customers who walk an average of 8,000 steps per day over a certain period. Steps are measured using a wearable device and an app the company created.

refund 「還付金」

special contract 「特約」

Dai-ichi Life Insurance Co. in March started a new special 30 contract that offers discounts of up to about 20 percent. Customers receive a discount just for submitting health exam results, and larger discounts are approved if certain

submit... 「～を提出する」

conditions are met.

Meiji Yasuda Life Insurance Co. is planning to offer a new product next April that provides partial premium refunds based on whether customers receive yearly health exams and ⁵ the results of these exams.

Still, some in the industry harbor concerns about these new products. "To reduce insurance premiums, we need deeper analyses of data to determine to what extent health-promoting activities such as exercise actually reduce the ¹⁰ incidence of disease," a senior executive at Nippon Life Insurance Co. said.

harbor concerns 「懸念を感じる」

to what extent 「どの程度」

The Japan News

● **Summary**
CD2-17

以下の空所 1 ～ 4 に当てはまる語を選択肢から選び、書き入れましょう。

As people (¹·   ) or avoid the typical milestones that spur them to take out insurance policies, insurance companies are betting on new health-dependent products to (²·   ) customers. These products offer discounts on insurance premiums depending on whether customers (³·   ) a variety of health checks and health-boosting activities. At the same time, some in the industry (⁴·   ) that such products will only make financial sense if the activities that are thought to promote health actually result in a lower incidence of disease.

warn	attract	complete	delay

● Comprehension 1

以下の1と2の条件に当てはまるある男性がそれぞれ生命保険に入りたいと考えている場合、あなたならどの会社の保険を薦めますか。当てはまるものをすべて選びましょう。

1. He believes exercise will not improve his fitness. （　　　　　　　）
2. He dislikes taking medical exams. （　　　　　　　）

    a. Sumitomo Life Insurance Co.

    b. Tokio Marine & Nichido Life Insurance Co.

    c. Dai-ichi Life Insurance Co.

    d. Meiji Yasuda Life Insurance Co.

● Comprehension 2

本文の内容に合うように、1と3の英文を完成させるのに適当なものを、2の質問の答えとして適当なものをa〜dから選びましょう。

1. Customers who sign up for Sumitomo's Vitality product but who earn only a small number of points will

    a. also be rewarded by additional discounts of up to 30 percent.

    b. still benefit from some amount of discount on their policy.

    c. end up paying more than if they had not signed up for the product.

    d. receive a monthly refund of ¥864 in addition to their discounts.

2. Why are the insurance companies encouraging customers to care for their health?

    a. They believe it will help to increase Japan's low birth rate.

    b. It provides additional opportunities to sell tech products like apps.

    c. Healthier customers might result in fewer health insurance claims.

    d. It is estimated that it will result in up to 8,000 new customers per day.

3. The senior executive at Nippon Life Insurance Co. is

    a. glad to see this new strategy being pursued across the sector.

    b. urging companies to find evidence to support some of their assumptions.

    c. anxious to see how customers will respond to these new products.

    d. concerned that some desperate customers will submit false medical reports.

Chapter 15

Stylish Sweden vs. Traditional India
巨大家具企業のインド進出

AFP/JIJI

● Key Expressions 1

CD2-18

音声を聞いて 1 〜 3 の（　　）内に適当な語を書き入れましょう。

1. In Hyderabad's bustling Nampally furniture market, customers (e _ _ _ _ _ _) a crowded and dusty labyrinth of shops.

ハイデラバードのにぎやかなナンパリー家具市場では、混雑してほこりっぽい迷路のような多数の店舗を客が探検している。

2. The Nampally Market is a (r _ _ _ _) to IKEA's Hyderabad store which opened six months ago.

ナンパリー市場は、6 か月前に開店したイケアのハイデラバード店の競争相手である。

3. A market analyst said that, within five years, IKEA hopes to capture 10 percent of India's furniture and home goods market (a _ _ _ _ _ _ _).

ある市場アナリストは、イケアは 5 年以内にインドの家具と家庭用品市場の年間 10 パーセントを獲得することを期待していると述べた。

以下の1～6の市場に関係する日本語の意味になるように、(　　)内に当てはまる語を選択肢から選び、書き入れましょう。

1. 市場アナリスト　　　　market (　　　　　　　　　　)
2. 市場競争力　　　　　　market (　　　　　　　　　　)
3. 平均株価　　　　　　　market (　　　　　　　　　　)
4. 消費者市場　　　　　　(　　　　　　　　　) market
5. 国内市場　　　　　　　(　　　　　　　　　) market
6. 露店市　　　　　　　　(　　　　　　　　　) market

consumer	domestic	average
street	analyst	competitiveness

接続詞 whether には、主に2つの用法があります。
①名詞節を形成:「～かどうか」の意味で、動詞・前置詞の目的語や、形式主語・形式目的語 it の意味上の主語・目的語になる。
②副詞節を形成:しばしば whether A or B の形で「A あるいは B だとしても」の意味になる。

日本語訳を参考に、以下の1～3の英文の [　　] 内の語句を並べかえましょう。

1. India is a test case [IKEA / should keep shifting resources / whether / for] toward emerging economies, including Latin America and China.
   インドは、イケアがラテンアメリカや中国を含む新興経済諸国に向けて資本を移動し続けるべきかどうかについてのテストケースとなっている。

2. It is [to Hyderabad's IKEA / not clear / all that foot traffic / whether] is translating to sales.
   ハイデラバードのイケアに対するあの客足のすべてが、販売につながるかどうかは明確ではない。

3. Whether IKEA [or in New Delhi / another store / opens / in Mumbai], demand for India's traditional custom-built furniture might remain high.
   イケアがムンバイあるいはニューデリーにさらに店舗をオープンするとしても、インドの伝統的な注文制作家具の需要は高いままかもしれない。

インドにおけるイケアの店舗拡大計画について、英文に<u>述べられていないもの</u>を1〜4から選びましょう。

IKEA plans to open its second India store this year in Mumbai, the financial capital, soon followed by Bengaluru, India's Silicon Valley, and the New Delhi national capital region.

By the time IKEA has built its planned 20 stores across India, it hopes to capture between 50 and 60 percent of the market.

"Two things that favor IKEA now: India's young population that is aspirational in nature and willing to experiment with brands from outside India, and the price point which is accessible to a wider segment of customers," a market analyst said.

The Associated Press

1. イケアがインドで次に出店するのはベンガルールとニューデリーであり、ムンバイはその後である。

2. イケアは、計画する20店舗の出店を終える頃までには、インドでの市場シェアが50〜60%となっていることを期待している。

3. ある市場アナリストによると、インドの若年層は海外ブランドを試すことに積極的である。

4. 同じアナリストが、イケアの価格設定はより広い消費者層が利用しやすいと語った。

● **Newspaper English**

 位置を示す副詞句（away... / from...など）や時間的順序を示す副詞節（after... / before...など）は、例えば two years after our graduation のように直前に具体的な数値情報を加えることで、読者により明確な情報やイメージを伝えられます。

日本語訳を参考に、以下の1と2の英文の下線部に当てはまる語句を書き入れましょう。

1. _____ IKEA opened its first store in Hyderabad, it is drawing between 10,000 and 30,000 visitors per day.

イケアがハイデラバードに最初の店舗をオープンした<u>6か月後</u>に、そこは1日1万人から3万人の客を引き寄せている。

2. Just _____ Hyderabad's IKEA, Nampally remains a beehive of activity.

ハイデラバードのイケアからほんの<u>20キロメートル離れた</u>ところにあるナンパリー（の市場）は、活気あふれた活動の場であり続けている。

woo... 「～に訴求する」

tap... 「～を開拓する」

haggle over prices 「値下げ交渉する」

made-to-order 「受注生産の」

tackle... 「～に立ち向かう」

given... 「～を考慮すれば」

saturation 「飽和」

recession 「景気後退」

expansion plan 「拡張計画」

cornucopia 「宝庫」

linens 「(寝具やテーブルクロスなどの) リネン類」

goodies 「商品」

Hitec City 「ハイテク・シティ」

cluster 「集合体」

sprout up 「(急激に) 出現する」

house... 「～に住居を提供する」

bite 「シェア」

novelty 「目新しさ」

IKEA woos India's rising consumer class, tapping new markets

HYDERABAD, India — In Hyderabad's bustling Nampally furniture market, customers explore a crowded, dusty labyrinth of shops, haggle over prices and work with carpenters to design made-to-order housewares.

This is the competition Swedish giant IKEA faces in 5 tackling the $40 billion Indian market for home furnishings, which is growing quickly along with the country's consumer class.

India is a test case for whether IKEA should keep shifting resources toward emerging economies, including Latin 10 America and China, given the saturation of markets in Europe and the United States — and the possibility of another global recession.

"India is an extremely important market for IKEA," said its Mumbai-based marketing manager Per Hornell. As one of 15 IKEA's biggest markets, India will be key to its overall expansion plans, he said.

Six months after IKEA opened its first store in Hyderabad, the 400,000-square-foot cornucopia of furniture, linens, kitchenware and other goodies is drawing between 10,000 20 and 30,000 visitors per day, Hornell said.

The store sits within Hyderabad's Hitec City, a cluster of global tech companies in the city of 6.7 million that includes Amazon, Google and Microsoft and employs hundreds of thousands of people. High-rise apartment buildings are 25 sprouting up to house the city's new migrants.

Just 20 kilometers (12 miles) from Hyderabad's IKEA, Nampally remains a beehive of activity — demand for India's traditional custom-built furniture remains high. But IKEA is already putting pressure on Indian furniture sellers' profits 30 and could eventually take a bigger bite of the market.

Apart from the novelty and comfort of its vast showrooms,

IKEA's offerings appeal to younger buyers not ready to invest in India's traditional heavy wood furniture.

But it is not clear whether all that foot traffic is translating to sales. "People here are out to enjoy. They are here more for entertainment than shopping for furniture," said Ranjitha Kumari, a software techie who brought her two kids one recent weekend. "It is not just a furniture shop. It is an experience which I think is difficult for others to recreate."

software techie「ソフトウェア技術者」

Forrester Research analyst Satish Meena said that, within five years, IKEA hopes to capture $4 billion annually — or 10 percent of India's furniture and home goods market.

Forrester Research「フォレスター・リサーチ（米国のリサーチ会社）」

The Associated Press

● **Summary** CD2-21

以下の空所 1 ～ 4 に当てはまる語を選択肢から選び、書き入れましょう。

A large Swedish furniture and houseware retailer, IKEA, is (1.   ) to expand its business into India. While demand for traditional, tailor-made furniture is still high, the company is hoping that India's younger, (2.   ) consumer class will be attracted to the retail experience and goods it is (3.   ). While customers are (4.   ) the new store in the thousands, it is still unclear whether this will translate into sales.

| offering | attempting | growing | visiting |

以下の１～４の英文の（　　）内に当てはまる国名を選択肢から選び、書き入れましょう。

1. (　　　　　　　　) is regarded as one of the world's emerging economies in East Asia.

2. (　　　　　　　　) is home to the headquarters of IKEA.

3. The home furnishings market in (　　　　　　　) has almost been saturated.

4. Many consumers in (　　　　　　　) still like traditional made-to-order furniture.

Sweden	India	China	the U.S.

本文の内容に合うように、１と２の英文を完成させるのに適当なものを、３の質問の答えとして適当なものをａ～ｄから選びましょう。

1. IKEA is using its Indian venture to assess

   a. the suitability of its products in different climates.

   b. the Nampally market as a possible site for a store.

   c. its likely success in other developing markets.

   d. its ability to adapt its products to reflect local tastes.

2. Per Hornell has noted that

   a. IKEA's success could be disastrous for small local businesses.

   b. the Indian market is crucial in terms of the company's growth.

   c. the number of people visiting the new store has fluctuated too widely.

   d. IKEA's current success will protect it from a global recession.

3. Which of the following statements about Ranjitha Kumari is true?

   a. She recently lost her children for a few moments in an IKEA store.

   b. She thinks Indian consumers are interested in quality, not shopping experience.

   c. She is wary of IKEA's effect on the local furniture industry.

   d. In her opinion, the store offers an experience that is difficult to copy.

Silent Speech Recognition App to Help People

音声不要の言語認識アプリ

The Asahi Shimbun

● Key Expressions 1

 CD2-22

音声を聞いて 1 ～ 3 の（　　）内に適当な語を書き入れましょう。

1. The app can (r _ _ _ _ _ _ _ _) particular words even when no sounds are produced.

そのアプリは、音声が発されなくても特定の語を認識することができる。

2. Those who would like to try the app are required to (r _ _ _ _ _ _ _) their name and address.

そのアプリを試してみたい人は、名前と住所を登録する必要がある。

3. The app could help conversations at noisy (c _ _ _ _ _ _ _ _ _ _ _) sites.

そのアプリは騒々しい建設現場での会話にも役立つことだろう。

名詞から派生した動詞を名詞派生動詞といいます。名詞・動詞それぞれの意味をおさえて、語彙力を増強しましょう。

以下の1〜5の日本語の意味をもつ名詞派生動詞を選択肢から選び、（　　　）内に書き入れましょう。

1. 〜に直面する　　　　　　　（　　　　　　　　）

2. 〜を声に出す　　　　　　　（　　　　　　　　）

3. 〜の見本（標本）をとる　　（　　　　　　　　）

4. 〜に向かう，行く　　　　　（　　　　　　　　）

5. 〜の議長を務める　　　　　（　　　　　　　　）

head	voice	sample	chair	face

日本語訳を参考に、以下の1〜3の英文の（　　　）中に当てはまる語句を選択肢から選び、書き入れましょう。

1. The researchers wanted to spread the lip-reading technology to (　　　　　　　　) possible.

研究者たちは、その読唇技術をできる限り多くの人々に広めたかった。

2. The lip-reading technology can recognize numbers from zero to nine (　　　　　　　　) 15 words and phrases

その読唇技術は、15個の単語やフレーズだけでなく、0から9までの数字も認識することができる。

3. It might take (　　　　　　　　　　　　　) ten years to achieve his goal.

彼の目標を達成するには、10年もの年月が必要かもしれない。

as long as	as many people as	as well as

岡山県のある病院での調査について、英文に述べられているものを1～4から選びましょう。

With the assistance of a hospital in Okayama, the research team employed a lip-reading app using artificial intelligence (AI) to analyze the lip movements of elderly people who had lost their voices. However, the correct recognition rate was considerably lower than for a sample of students.

The results appear to be attributable to the difference in how young people move their lips compared with older people, the team said.

Such issues are expected to be resolved by having the AI learn from a larger data set.

The Asahi Shimbun

Note attributable to... 「～のせいである」

1. 読唇アプリを用いて、まず発声に問題のない高齢者の唇の動きから分析した。
2. 高齢者の唇の動きのサンプルの認識率は、学生のそれと比べて大幅に低かった。
3. 高齢者の唇の動きと学生の唇の動きの間に、目立った違いは認められなかった。
4. AIにより多くのデータを与えても、高齢者の認識率が改善するとは考えにくい。

● **Newspaper English**

〈with＋目的語＋形容詞に相当する語句（分詞句・前置詞句など）〉の形式で用いるwithの用法は「（目的語）を～しながら」「（目的語）を～したままで」といった意味を表します。コンパクトに情報を盛り込むことができるため、英字新聞でも頻繁に活用されます。

日本語訳を参考に、以下の1と2の英文の［　］内の語句を正しい語順に並びかえましょう。

1. Collecting samples from a wide variety of people is one of the objectives of the study, with [to / the app / being offered] the public.
   そのアプリを一般に公開して、さまざまな人々からサンプルを収集することがその研究目的の一つである。

2. The journalist filmed the attempt with [attached / a camera / to] his helmet.
   そのジャーナリストはカメラがヘルメットに装着された状態でその試みを撮影した。

AI-powered app gives voice to people with speech disabilities

powered by... 「〜を搭載した」
enunciate... 「〜を明確に発音する」
facilitate... 「〜を容易にする、手助けする」
speech disorder 「発話障害」

An app powered by artificial intelligence (AI) that can read speakers' lips even if they do not enunciate words is available for those willing to collaborate in a study aimed at facilitating smooth conversation for people with speech disorders. Collecting samples from a wide variety of people is 5 one of the objectives of the study, with the app being offered to the public to spread the lip-reading technology to as many people as possible.

the Kyushu Institute of Technology 「九州工業大学」

The lip-reading AI technology, developed by Takeshi Saitoh, Associate Professor of intelligence information studies 10 at the Kyushu Institute of Technology, can recognize numbers from zero to nine as well as 15 words and phrases such as "a-ri-ga-to-u" (thank you) and "ha-ji-me-ma-shi-te" (nice to meet you) in the study. The app analyzes video of the movements of 20 facial landmarks around the mouth of the 15 speaker and uses these movements to estimate the syllables and thus the most probable word.

facial landmark 「(顔面の) 目印となる場所」
estimate... 「〜を推定する」
syllable 「音節」

For example, when the app interprets syllables as "a, i, ga, to, u," it can figure out that the correct word is "a-ri-ga-to-u" because "a, i, ga, to, u" has no meaning in Japanese. 20

feed... into 「〜を読み込ませる、入力する」

As it only analyzes lip movements, the app can recognize particular words even when no sounds are produced. Using data collected from 48 students and fed into the AI, the research group achieved a correct recognition rate of 71 percent. 25

larynx cancer 「喉頭がん」
feel frustrated 「もどかしさを感じる」

People who have lost their voices owing to larynx cancer or other reasons can feel frustrated or lonely, as, while they are still able to move their lips, they are unable to speak, according to Saitoh.

He aims to develop a technology that enables people with 30 difficulties voicing words to have smooth conversations.

When those who have lost their voice move their lips in

front of the camera of a smartphone, Saitoh's dream technology will allow AI to swiftly read the movements and turn them into sounds to be played over a speaker.

swiftly「素早く」

5 The technology can be applied to other settings and systems, such as car navigation devices otherwise hindered from recognizing a driver's instructions owing to noise, such as music and conversation among passengers.

setting「状況、環境」

hinder「妨げる」

The Asahi Shimbun

● Summary

以下の空所 1 〜 4 に当てはまる語を選択肢から選び、書き入れましょう。

New (1.   ) being developed by a Japanese researcher may one day aid smooth communication for those who have (2.   ) producing sounds from their mouths and others who find themselves in noisy environments. In the form of an app, the technology analyzes movements around the (3.   ) of a speaker, using this data to produce an interpretation of the syllables and thus predict the most likely word. The researcher is currently collecting more sample data in order to improve the (4.   ) of the artificial intelligence that drives the app.

| technology | accuracy | mouth | difficulty |

以下の 1 ～ 4 の英文について、本文の内容に合うものには T（True）を、合わないものには F（False）を（　　）内に書き入れましょう。

1. Mr. Saitoh has a speech disorder. （　　）

2. The lip-reading app can recognize words only when sounds are produced.

（　　）

3. The data fed into the AI was collected from students. （　　）

4. The lip-reading technology has already been applied to a car navigation system. （　　）

本文の内容に合うように、1 と 3 の英文を完成させるのに適当なものを、2 の質問の答えとして適当なものを a ～ d から選びましょう。

1. Associate Professor Saitoh wants many people to use the app in order to
　a. raise funding for its further development.
　b. gather more data for the AI to learn from.
　c. find more people living with speech disorders.
　d. familiarize the public with AI technology.

2. In total, how many different numbers can the app currently recognize?
　a. 0
　b. 9
　c. 10
　d. 25

3. Saitoh predicts that the app could be of use to
　a. people who are no longer able to voice sounds due to illness.
　b. surgeons working with throat cancer patients.
　c. manufacturers that produce speakers for smartphones.
　d. passengers who cannot hear car navigation instructions.

Chapter 17

Real vs. Artificial Christmas Trees

本物かどうか—それが問題だ

Aflo

● Key Expressions 1

CD2-26

音声を聞いて1～3の（　）内に適当な語を書き入れましょう。

1. Many people in the USA put up and (d _ _ _ _ _ _ _) Christmas trees during the Christmas holiday season.

アメリカ合衆国では、多くの人々がクリスマス休暇の間、クリスマスツリーを置き、飾り付ける。

2. Between 75 and 80 percent of Americans who get a Christmas tree choose an (a _ _ _ _ _ _ _ _ _) one these days.

クリスマスツリーを入手するアメリカ人の75～80パーセントが、最近ではフェイクツリー（人工のツリー）を選ぶ。

3. Small Christmas tree farms that allow families to cut their own (e _ _ _ _ _ _ _ _ _) remain popular.

家族に自分たちの常緑樹（の木）を切らせてくれる小規模クリスマスツリー農家は根強い人気がある。

-ity は、性質や状態などを表す接尾辞です。主として形容詞の語尾に付き、その形容詞の持つ特性を表す名詞を形成します。

枠内の説明を参考に、以下の 1 〜 6 の形容詞を -ity を含む名詞にしましょう。

1. diverse（多様な）　　→[　　　　　　　　] （多様性）
2. mature（成熟した、十分に成長した）
　　　　　　　　　　　　→[　　　　　　　　] （成熟、十分な成長）
3. real（現実の）　　　→[　　　　　　　　] （現実性）
4. original（独自の）　→[　　　　　　　　] （独自性）
5. similar（類似の）　→[　　　　　　　　] （類似性）
6. vital（生命の、元気な）→[　　　　　　　　] （生命力、元気、活力）

日本語訳を参考に、以下の 1 〜 3 の英文の （　　） 内に当てはまる語句を選択肢から選び、書き入れましょう。

1. Christmas trees made of plastic are getting popular since they can be reused year （　　　　　　） year.
   プラスチック製のクリスマスツリーが人気になっているのは、毎年毎年再使用することができるからである。

2. It is difficult to predict demand for real Christmas trees years （　　　　　　　）.
   何年も先の本物のクリスマスツリーの需要を予測することは困難だ。

3. Evergreen trees retain green leaves all year （　　　　　　　）.
   常緑樹は、一年中緑の葉を保ち続ける。

round	after	out

最近クリスマスツリーを購入したシャックルトンさんについて、英文に述べられているものを１〜４から選びましょう。

Denise Shackleton got a real Christmas tree each season before switching to an artificial one. On a recent day, she was at an artificial tree outlet store in Burlingame, California, shopping for a new tree for herself and one for her daughter.

"No one got as excited about a real tree as me, but it was just too much work to put the real tree on my car, get it into the house — all of that," she said. "It's totally for convenience."

The Associated Press

1. フェイクツリーの品質がよくなり、本物のツリーの必要性を感じなくなった。
2. 最近、カルフォルニア州のアウトレットストアでフェイクツリーを２本購入した。
3. 昔から、本物のツリーを飾ることに対するこだわりはあまり持っていなかった。
4. ツリー農家が自宅まで配達してくれるなら、本物を購入してもよいと思っている。

● Newspaper English

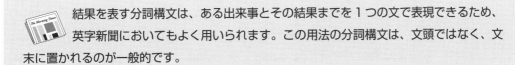

結果を表す分詞構文は、ある出来事とその結果までを１つの文で表現できるため、英字新聞においてもよく用いられます。この用法の分詞構文は、文頭ではなく、文末に置かれるのが一般的です。

日本語訳を参考に、以下の１と２の英文の［　　］内の語句を正しい語順に並びかえましょう。

1. Christmas tree farmers are worried that young adults starting their own family traditions will opt for an artificial tree, [of customers / farmers / a generation / costing].
   これから自分たちの家族の習慣を始めようとしている若い人たちがフェイクツリーを選び、その結果一世代分の顧客を失うことになることを、クリスマスツリー農家は懸念している。

2. The typhoon struck the island, [mudslides / causing / and / floods].
   台風がその島に上陸し、洪水や土砂崩れを引き起こした。

It's Christmas. Keep It Real.

Christmas tree farmers across the U.S. worry people buying real trees are slowly dwindling. Artificial trees, once crude imitations of an evergreen, are now so realistic that it is hard to tell they are fakes, even though many are conveniently pre-strung with lights and can fold up for 5 storage at the push of a button.

Between 75 and 80 percent of Americans who get a Christmas tree now choose an artificial one, and the $1 billion market for fake trees is growing at about 4 percent a year. 10

To combat this trend, Christmas tree farmers have joined forces as the Christmas Tree Promotion Board and are running a social media ad campaign to tout the benefits of a real evergreen. The campaign is called "It's Christmas. Keep It Real!" 15

A series of short movies on Instagram and Facebook show real families hunting for the perfect tree, cutting it down and decorating it. The target audience is the "millennial mom" because tree farmers are increasingly worried that young adults starting their own family traditions will opt for an 20 artificial tree, costing farmers a generation of customers.

To fourth-generation tree farmer Casey Grogan, that angst is as real as the towering noble and Nordmann firs he grows at Silver Bells Tree Farm in Silverton, Oregon. Oregon is the nation's No. 1 producer of Christmas trees, yet Grogan 25 says he has watched about half the fellow tree farmers around him go out of business in the past decade.

A seedling takes 8 to 10 years to grow to maturity, and it is difficult to predict demand years out, he said. He harvested about half as many trees this year as he did a decade ago, 30 and with every new seedling he plants this season, he knows he is taking a gamble that the demand will still be there in 2028.

dwindle「徐々に減少する」

pre-strung with lights「ライトをあらかじめ巻き付けて」
storage「収納」

tout...「〜を（大げさに）宣伝する」

angst「不安、懸念」
noble fir「ノーブルモミ」
Nordmann fir「ノードマンモミ」

seedling「苗」

"We're an industry that would like to remain here and be around — and if everybody buys an artificial tree, we're not going to be here," said Grogan. "It may be a little difficult, but not everything is easy," he added of buying a real tree. "It's
5 worth the extra effort."

The Associated Press

● Summary

○ CD2-29

以下の空所 1 〜 4 に当てはまる語を選択肢から選び、書き入れましょう。

As more and more American families choose (1.   ) Christmas trees over (2.   ) ones, the nation's Christmas tree farmers are worrying for their livelihoods. The problem is made worse by the fact that trees take (3.   ) years to mature, meaning that the farmers have to take risks as they try to predict demand so far in advance. In an attempt to solve the issue, farmers are working together to promote real trees on (4.   ) media.

| social | artificial | many | real |

● Comprehension 1

クリスマスツリー振興委員会（Christmas Tree Promotion Board）について、本文の内容に当てはまるものには T（True）を、当てはまらないものには F（False）を（　）内に書き入れましょう。

1. It was established by artificial Christmas tree manufacturers and retailers.

（　　）

2. It is taking advantage of social media to promote real evergreen Christmas trees.

（　　）

3. Not only Christmas tree farmers, but also artificial tree retailers belong to it.

（　　）

4. It offers financial advice to Christmas tree farmers and families. （　　）

● Comprehension 2

本文の内容に合うように、1〜3の英文を完成させるのに適当なものを a 〜 d から選びましょう。

1. According to the article, artificial trees are now so realistic that
   a. they do not even require lights to look attractive.
   b. customers sometimes forget they can be folded up.
   c. people find it difficult to identify them as fake trees.
   d. they can be made to get smaller with age.

2. The "millennial mom" is
   a. a woman who has become Casey Grogan's best customer over the years.
   b. the title of the person who heads the Christmas Tree Promotion Board.
   c. the name given to the typical consumer to whom the tree farmers are appealing.
   d. a person who famously stopped buying real Christmas trees around 2000.

3. Casey Grogan wants to convince people that
   a. trees from Oregon are the best in the country.
   b. farming Christmas trees can still be profitable.
   c. artificial trees do not look as good as real ones.
   d. the difficulty in getting a real tree is worth it.

Chapter 18

Take them to the Ski Resort
グローバルなスキーバブル

The Yomiuri Shimbun

● **Key Expressions 1**　

音声を聞いて1〜3の（　）内に適当な語を書き入れましょう。

1. Foreign tourists are (i _ _ _ _ _ _ _ _ _ _ _) visiting ski resorts in Japan because they want to enjoy skiing on "Japow."
   "ジャパウ" の上でスキーを楽しみたいために、日本のスキーリゾートを訪れる外国人観光客が増加している。

2. "Japow" is the nickname of Japan's (p _ _ _ _ _) snow famous for its high quality.
   "ジャパウ" とは、高品質で有名な日本のパウダースノーの愛称である。

3. To deal with this influx of visitors from overseas, many areas are providing more information in foreign languages and hiring (m _ _ _ _ _ _ _ _ _ _ _) staff.
   この海外からの客の殺到に対応するため、多くのスキー場では外国語での情報をさらに多く提供し、多言語を使うことができるスタッフを雇用している。

● Key Expressions 2

triple「3倍にする、3倍になる」は、数字の3を示すラテン語 "tres" を語源に持ちます。同様に、ラテン語で数を表す "unus"=1、"duo"=2、"quattuor"=4 などを語源とする英単語も多数あります。

枠内の説明を参考に、以下の1〜5の日本語に該当する語を選択肢から選び、（　　）内に書き入れましょう。

1. 複製をつくる　　　　　（　　　　　　　　　）
2. 年4回の　　　　　　　（　　　　　　　　　）
3. （カメラの）三脚　　　（　　　　　　　　　）
4. 統一する　　　　　　　（　　　　　　　　　）
5. 唯一の　　　　　　　　（　　　　　　　　　）

quarterly	unique	unify	tripod	duplicate

● Key Expressions 3

日本語訳を参考に、以下の1〜3の英文の（　　）内の語を適当な形に変化させ、「数の増加や量の拡大を表す表現」を完成させましょう。

1. Businesses and municipalities are trying to increase overseas visitors, and also hoping (lift →　　　　　　　　　　) domestic demand.
企業や自治体は、海外からの旅行者を増加させる努力をしており、また国内の需要を増大させることも期待している。

2. "We hope that awareness of the area will (boost →　　　　　　　　　) overseas," said the general director of Inbound Tourism Promotion at the Akita prefectural government.
「私たちは、このスキー場の認知が海外で高まることを希望しています」と、秋田県観光振興課課長は述べた。

3. Large resorts in Hokkaido and Nagano Prefecture have (see →　　　　　　　　) a sharp rise in visitors not only from Western but also from Asian countries.
北海道や長野県の大規模なリゾート地では、西洋諸国だけではなく、アジア諸国からの旅行者が急激な増加をしている。

バックカントリースキー（整備されたゲレンデではない自然の山を滑るスキー）について、英文に<u>述べられていないもの</u>を 1 〜 4 から選びましょう。

As the popularity of "backcountry" skiing on natural slopes outside ski-area boundaries has increased, so has the occurrence of accidents linked to the activity. Some ski resorts have created their own rules for backcountry skiing, such as requiring people to submit routes beforehand or pay rescue fees.

"Businesses and municipalities need to create an environment that reduces the risk of accidents and allows skiers to have fun," said an expert.

The Japan News

1. バックカントリースキーの人気が高まるにつれて、関連する事故も増えている。
2. バックカントリースキーに関する独自の規則を策定するスキー場もある。
3. スキー場が定める規制には、スキールートの事前提出をスキーヤーに義務づけることなどが含まれる。
4. 専門家によると、企業や自治体は事故のリスクを抑制するよう自然環境の維持管理をする必要がある。

● **Newspaper English**

新聞記事では「数」に関する情報が有効なため、主語が〈a number of ＋複数名詞〉の形を取ることがしばしばあります。large/small/growing など様々な形容詞を加えて a large number of people（大勢の人々）といった使い方ができます（この場合の主語は複数扱い）。一方、the number of...（〜の数）が主語になる時は、原則として単数扱いとなることに注意しましょう。

日本語訳を参考に、以下の 1 〜 3 の英文の（　　）内に当てはまる語を枠内から選んで書き入れ、また動詞を適当な形に変えましょう。

1. A (　　　　　　　　　) number of foreign tourists [be → 　　　　　] visiting Japan's ski resorts.
   日本のスキーリゾートを訪れる外国人観光客がますます増加している。

2. A (　　　　　　　　　) number of foreign tourists [be → 　　　　　] visiting Japan's ski resorts.
   多くの外国人観光客が、日本のスキーリゾートを訪れている。

3. (　　　　　　　　　) number of Japanese people visiting domestic ski resorts [be → 　　　　] declining.
   国内のスキーリゾートを訪れる日本人の数が減少している。

Overseas visitors lift winter tourism

The number of foreign tourists visiting Japan's ski resorts is increasing despite a continued slump in the domestic ski and snowboard industries. Businesses and municipalities are trying to accelerate the increase of overseas visitors, while also hoping to lift domestic demand. 5

"That was my first time out on the snow. I had a lot of fun, even without skiing," said Melissa Crowley, a South African studying at Akita University, after riding on an inflatable raft pulled by a snowmobile.

Crowley took part in a trial-run of a tour for foreigners to 10 a defunct ski area. It was organized by a private company and the town of Senboku, Akita prefecture.

"We hope awareness of the area will be boosted overseas and that the tour will be able to operate as a private business beginning next season," said Kazuhide Masuko, general 15 director of Inbound Tourism Promotion at the Akita prefectural government.

The Japan Tourism Agency hopes that this kind of initiative will help to increase the number of repeat and long-term visitors. The agency is funding related surveys and it 20 plans to promote similar programs nationwide.

Japan's high-quality powder snow, dubbed Japow, is well-known overseas. Large resorts in Hokkaido and Nagano Prefecture have seen a sharp rise in visitors from China and other Asian countries in addition to tourists from Australia, 25 Europe and the United States.

The number of foreign tourists who visit Japan to ski or snowboard has more than tripled since 2012, increasing from about 277,000 to about 858,000 in 2017, according to agency estimates. To deal with this influx, many areas are providing 30 more information in foreign languages and hiring multilingual staff.

Other facilities are trying to differentiate themselves

---

inflatable raft 「(スノーラフティング用の) ゴムボート」

trial-run 「試験、試行」

defunct 「廃れた」

the Japan Tourism Agency 「観光庁」

initiative 「取り組み」

fund... 「～に資金提供をする」

A, dubbed B 「Bと呼ばれるA」

estimate 「推計」

differentiate... 「～を差別化する」

while eyeing the domestic market, introducing measures such as restricting the use of snowboards to attract older skiers or providing family-friendly facilities such as rooms where mothers can breastfeed their babies.

5   Yama-Kei Publishers Co., based in Chiyoda Ward, Tokyo, revived two ski magazines for the first time in seven seasons in 2015. The launch of a third publication is planned for later this year. "If ski areas make themselves more attractive and people learn about the appeal of the area as a whole,
10 domestic customers will return," said Kazuki Hisada, an editor at the publisher.

The Japan News

eye... 「～に注目する」

measure 「方策」

breastfeed ... 「～に授乳する」

Yama-Kei Publishers Co. 「株式会社山と渓谷社」

revive... 「～を復刊させる」

● Summary   CD2-33

以下の空所 1 ～ 4 に当てはまる語を選択肢から選び、書き入れましょう。

Amid a downturn in the number of domestic (1.   ) visiting Japan's winter sport resorts, (2.   ) promoting tourism have launched various (3.   ) in an attempt to turn the market around. Programs include promoting the resorts to foreign tourists and offering differentiated (4.   ) and facilities designed to attract older people and families.

| agencies | tourists | initiatives | areas |

本文に述べられているスキーヤー誘致策の中で、主に外国人観光客向けのものにはFを、主に国内客向けのものにはDを、以下の1〜4の（　　）内に書き入れましょう。

1. To provide breastfeeding facilities for parents （　　）
2. To organize a special tour for participants to enjoy "Japow" （　　）
3. To employ staff who can use several languages （　　）
4. To make slopes safe for elderly users （　　）

本文の内容に合うように、1と2の質問の答えとして適当なものを、3の英文を完成させるのに適当なものをa〜dから選びましょう。

1. Which phrase best describes the recent trend in domestic tourists visiting Japan's ski resorts?
   a. An ongoing decline
   b. A sudden fall
   c. A steady increase
   d. A fast rise

2. According to the article, what happened in Akita?
   a. A Japanese rode an inflatable raft on the snow for the first time.
   b. An international student started her own ski rental business.
   c. The municipality took the case against a local business to trial.
   d. A business and the local government collaborated on a project.

3. The article suggests that
   a. the quality of Japanese snow is a mystery outside of the country.
   b. the number of foreign languages used at ski resorts has tripled.
   c. a stricter regulation on the use of snowboards might lure older skiers.
   d. Japanese families have been put off by too many foreign tourists.

Chapter 19

Impossible Made Possible

肉なしバーガー"増食"中

Aflo

● **Key Expressions 1**　　　　　　　　　　　　　　◎ CD2-34

音声を聞いて1～3の（　　）内に適当な語を書き入れましょう。

1. Burger King announced it was testing out Impossible Whoppers, made with plant-based patties, in 59 (l _ _ _ _ _ _ _ _) in Missouri.
   バーガーキングは、植物を使ったパティで作ったインポッシブル・ワッパーの試験販売をミズーリ州の 59 店舗で行うと発表した。

2. The burger giant is working in (c _ _ _ _ _ _ _ _ _ _ _ _) with Impossible Foods, which supplies patties used to cook healthier meatless burgers.
   このバーガー業界の巨人は、より健康的な肉なしバーガーを調理するために使われるパティを供給するインポッシブル・フーズと提携して業務を行っている。

3. With attention to (a _ _ _ _ _ _ _ _ _ _) meats growing, the two companies expect to expand the offering nationwide in the near future.
   代用肉への注目が高まっていることを受けて、両社は近い将来、この商品提供を（米）国全域に拡大するつもりである。

-er, -or は動詞に付いて「〜する人・組織」の意味を表す接尾辞です。-ee はその行為・動作を「受ける人・組織」の意味になる接尾辞です。

以下の1〜6の日本語に該当する語になるように、選択肢から適当な動詞を選び、枠内からいずれかの接尾辞をつけて（　）内に書き入れましょう。

1. フランチャイズ加盟者　（　　　　　　　　　　　　　　）

2. 雇用主　　　　　　　　（　　　　　　　　　　　　　　）

3. 編集者　　　　　　　　（　　　　　　　　　　　　　　）

4. 研修生　　　　　　　　（　　　　　　　　　　　　　　）

5. 面接を受ける人　　　　（　　　　　　　　　　　　　　）

6. 審判員　　　　　　　　（　　　　　　　　　　　　　　）

| interview | edit | employ | refer | train | franchise |

日本語訳を参考に、以下の1〜3の英文の（　）内に当てはまる語を選び、必要なら形を変えて書き入れましょう。

1. On April 1, Burger King released a (　　　　　　　　　　)-camera-style promotion video on the web featuring plant-based Whoppers instead of meat.
バーガーキングは4月1日に、肉の代わりに植物を使ったワッパーを取り上げた隠しカメラ的なプロモーション映像をウェブで公開した。

2. A genetically (　　　　　　　　　　) yeast creates the key ingredient, which makes the patties apparently bleed like real meat.
遺伝子組み換え酵母が重要な成分を生み出し、それによってパティを本物の肉のように肉汁が出るようにする。

3. In January 2019, Los Angeles-(　　　　　　　　　　) Beyond Meat announced it was launching its plant-based burger at fast-food chain Carl's Jr.
2019年1月に、ロサンゼルスを拠点とするビヨンド・ミートはファストフードチェーンのカールスジュニアで植物を使ったバーガーを発売することを発表した。

| base | hide | modify |

植物を使った代用肉製品の販売状況について、英文に<u>述べられていないもの</u>を１〜４から選びましょう。

Last year, total U.S. retail sales of plant-based meat substitutes grew over 23 percent to exceed $760 million, according to Nielsen sales data analyzed by The Good Food Institute, a non-profit promoting plant-based alternatives to animal products.

Burger King rivals, food conglomerates and meat packers are cooking up more plant-based burgers. McDonald's Corp., the world's biggest fast-food chain, sells soy-based burgers in Finland and Sweden.

Reuters

1. 昨年、米国全土での代用肉製品の売上は７億６千万ドルを超えた。
2. 売上データの基になる分析は、食肉の代わりに植物を使った製品を奨励する NPO が行った。
3. バーガーキングの競合企業や他の会社が、植物を使ったバーガーのレシピを公開しようとしている。
4. 北欧ではマクドナルドの大豆バーガーが販売されている。

● **Newspaper English**

 産業界のニュース記事では、しばしば〈企業名＋ announce ＋名詞句 / 名詞節〉という定型表現が使用されます。この表現は、企業自体が独自に発信するニュース・リリース（news release）でも多用されます。

日本語訳を参考に、以下の１と２の英文の ［　　］ 内の語句を並べかえましょう。

1. On Monday, Burger King [the Impossible Whopper in / the rollout of / 59 stores in / announced] and around St. Louis, Missouri.

___

バーガーキングは月曜日に、ミズーリ州セントルイスおよびその周辺の 59 店舗でインポッシブル・ワッパーの発売をしたと発表した。

2. In December, Impossible Foods [with the mission of / announced that / plant-based alternatives / it is currently developing] replacing all food animals by 2035.

___

インポッシブル・フーズは 12 月に、2035 年までにあらゆる食用動物に取って代わることを目標として、植物を使った代用品の開発を現在進めていると発表した。

'Impossible' meatless patty gets Burger King Whopper test

Vegetarian burgers may finally be getting the recognition they need to go mainstream. On Monday, Burger King and Silicon Valley startup Impossible Foods announced the rollout of the Impossible Whopper in 59 stores in and around St. Louis, Missouri. 5

To mark the launch on April Fool's Day, the burger giant released a hidden-camera-style promo video showing the serving of plant-based Whoppers instead of meat to customers who marvel that they cannot tell the difference.

marvel「驚嘆する」

live up to...「〜にかなう」

"We wanted to make sure we had something that lived up 10 to the expectations of the Whopper," said Burger King's North America president, Christopher Finazzo. "We've done sort of a blind taste test with our franchisees, with people in the office, with my partners on the executive team, and virtually nobody can tell the difference." 15

executive team「経営陣」

The Impossible Whopper comes at an extra cost — about a dollar more than the beef patty Whopper. But Finazzo said research shows consumers are willing to pay more for the plant-based burger.

Plant-based meat substitutes have been gaining 20 popularity as more attention is focused on the environmental hazards of industrial ranching. Finazzo said his research shows customers mainly like it for the health benefits. The Impossible Burger patty has zero cholesterol.

industrial ranching「工業型畜産」

cholesterol「コレステロール」

Impossible Foods, based in Redwood City, California, 25 launched its first faux meat patty over two years ago. A genetically modified yeast creates the key ingredient, called heme, which makes the patties appear to bleed and taste like real meat.

faux meat patty「代用肉パティ」

heme「ヘム（生体内に存在する鉄の化合物）」

serve up...「〜を提供する」

Burger King is not the first to serve up a no-meat burger. 30 Los Angeles-based Beyond Meat in early January announced it was rolling out its plant-based burger at fast-food chain

Carl's Jr.

Finazzo said Burger King also researched Beyond Meat, but decided that Impossible Foods' offering was a better fit. "Around the taste, around the brand recognition, around the
5 price, all those things were important factors in choosing Impossible," he said.

Impossible Foods tailored a patty specifically for the Whopper, Chief Executive Pat Brown said. "We're now in well over 6,000 restaurants. If the Burger King launch is as
10 successful as I expect it to be, and we go nationwide, that will add more than 7,000 restaurants that serve the Impossible Burger."

tailor... specifically 「〜を特別な仕上がりにする」

Chief Executive (Officer) = CEO

Reuters

● Summary   ◎ CD2-37

以下の空所 1 〜 4 に当てはまる語を選択肢から選び、書き入れましょう。

A number of (1.   ) chains in the United States have entered into partnerships with manufacturers of (2.   ) burgers in order to meet growing demand for meatless options. Very few people can tell the difference between a (3.   ) patty and these new alternatives. Moreover, despite a slightly higher price, they remain appealing to (4.   ) consumers.

| plant-based | health-conscious | meat-based | fast-food |

以下の１〜３の英文の（　）内に当てはまる企業名を選択肢から選び、書き入れましょう。なお、複数回使う企業名もあります。

1. (   ) uses a GM yeast to produce heme, which makes a no-meat burger taste just like a real beef burger.

2. (   ) started supplying a rival fast-food chain of

(   ) with meatless patties in January 2019.

3. Before the release of its plant-based burger, (   ) conducted a blind taste test with its staff and affiliates.

| Burger King | Impossible Foods | Beyond Meat |

本文の内容に合うように、１の英文を完成させるのに適当なものを、２と３の質問の答えとして適当なものを a 〜 d から選びましょう。

1. Burger King timed the release of its Impossible Whopper to coincide with

a. the release of a similar product by one of its rivals.

b. a well-known annual celebration of practical jokes.

c. major investment from a Silicon Valley startup.

d. a new law in Missouri that makes meat more expensive.

2. Which of the following statements about Christopher Finazzo is true?

a. He finds that almost no one around him can tell a non-meat burger from a beef-based one.

b. He believes customers are happy to pay extra for a bigger patty.

c. He has some doubts about the health dangers of eating meat.

d. He says it is only a matter of time before industrial ranching is outlawed.

3. Which of the following statements about Impossible Foods is true?

a. Burger King is their first client.

b. They developed a new product for Burger King.

c. Beyond Meat is their parent company.

d. They declined an offer from Carl's Jr.

Chapter 20

Yet Another Step of the Giant

ネット企業の新たなフロンティア

©Christian Delbert | Dreamstim.com (left) / ©Radub85 | Dreamstim.com (right)

● **Key Expressions 1** ◎ CD2-38

音声を聞いて１～３の（　　）内に適当な語を書き入れましょう。

1. U.S. internet giants have been trying to move into the health industry since identifying it as an untapped (m _ _ _ _ _).

米国のネット関連巨大企業が、ヘルスケア業界を未開拓な市場であると見なし、その業界への参入を試みている。

2. Beth Israel Deaconess Medical Center, in (p _ _ _ _ _ _ _ _ _ _) with Amazon, analyzed data from surgeries at the hospital to develop a new reservation system.

ベス・イスラエル・ディーコネス・メディカルセンターはアマゾンと共同で、新たな予約システムを開発するために、この病院での手術データを分析した。

3. Amazon's tools are now helping the medical center book operating room time more precisely to expand (c _ _ _ _ _ _ _) by 30 percent.

アマゾンの装置は現在、そのメディカルセンターが手術室をより正確に予約することに役立ちつつあり、受け入れ能力が30％増加している。

● Key Expressions 2

頭字語（acronym）は、語群を構成する各語の先頭の文字や音節をつないだ略語です。簡略で便利なため、元の語句よりも使用頻度が高くなる場合もあります。

日本語を参考に、以下の1〜5の頭字語の元になっている語句を下の選択肢から選び、（　　）内に書き入れましょう。

1. AI　　（　　　　　　）（　　　　　　　　）［人工知能］
2. OR　　（　　　　　　）（　　　　　　　　）［手術室］
3. ICU　（　　　　　）（　　　　　　）（　　　　　　　　）［集中治療室］
4. AED　（　　　　　）（　　　　　　）（　　　　　　）

［自動体外式除細動器］
5. GAFA　（　　　　　）（　　　　　　）（　　　　　　）（　　　　　　）

［ガーファ］

Amazon	Apple	artificial	automated	care	external
defibrillator	Facebook	Google	intelligence	intensive	
operating	room	unit			

● Key Expressions 3

対比や比較、並列を表す構文には、接続詞や比較級を用いるものなど、さまざまな種類があります。以下の1と2の英文の（　　）内に当てはまる語を選択肢から選び、書き入れましょう。ただし、文頭に来る語も小文字で与えられています。

1. Alexa will (　　　　　　) be replacing doctors anytime soon, (　　　　　　) Amazon says AI can help hospitals become more efficient.

アレクサ［注：アマゾンが開発した AI アシスタント］は近い将来、医師に取って代わるわけではないが、AI が病院をより効率的にすることに役立つ可能性があるとアマゾンは述べている。

2. (　　　　　　　) the tech industry has high hopes that powerful computing tools can improve diagnoses and treatment, Beth Israel Deaconess' first projects with Amazon are (　　　　　　) about sophisticated therapies and (　　　　　　) about making day-to-day tasks more cost-effective.

強力な計算装置が診断や治療を改善できるという高い期待をハイテク業界が持っている一方で、ベス・イスラエル・ディーコネスによるアマゾンとの最初の取り組みは、先端的な治療法に関するというよりも、日常業務をより費用対効果の高いものにすることについてのものである。

less	not	while	more	but

ベス・イスラエル・ディーコネス・メディカルセンターとアマゾンが共同開発中の AI アプリについて、英文に<u>述べられていないもの</u>を 1 〜 4 から選びましょう。

Beth Israel Deaconess and Amazon engineers analyzed anonymous data from surgeries at the hospital going back to the 1980s. They have developed and tested the new scheduling system over the past two years. The system lets doctors reserve operating time as easily as booking restaurants on OpenTable. "We have an app that a physician can now use by saying something like 'I'd like to schedule for tomorrow morning at 7:30, appendectomy,'" said an executive in charge.

Bloomberg

Note   appendectomy「虫垂除去手術」

1. ベス・イスラエル・ディーコネスとアマゾンの技術者は、1980 年代以降の手術に関する匿名データを分析した。
2. 彼らは新たな予約システムを過去 2 年にわたって開発・試行してきた。
3. その OpenTable というシステムを使って、医師は手術室だけでなく病院の食堂の予約も可能である。
4. 担当理事によると、医師が日時と手術内容をアプリに告げることで予約は完了する。

● Newspaper English

巨大な企業・組織がニュースで取り上げられる際、その巨大さを読者や視聴者に印象づけるため、しばしば体の大きな動物（mammoth、gorilla など）や架空の生物（giant、behemoth［旧約聖書の『ヨブ記』に登場する動物］など）に例えられます。本拠地名や業界の分野を示す語が先行することもしばしばあります。

以下の 1 〜 3 の英文の下線部と置きかえられる企業名を a 〜 c から選びましょう。

1. <u>The Seattle-based tech behemoth</u> gave the Harvard Medical School teaching hospital a grant valued at as much as $2 million. (   )
2. <u>Japan's auto giant</u> finally unveiled a new hybrid vehicle at Tokyo Motor Show. (   )
3. <u>The furniture mammoth</u> plans to further expand its business in India. (   )

a. Toyota   **b.** IKEA   **c.** Amazon

Amazon gives AI to Harvard hospital in tech's latest health push

push「動き」

Alexa will not be replacing doctors anytime soon, but Amazon says artificial intelligence can help hospitals become more efficient.

Amazon Web Services unit
「アマゾン・ウェブ・サービシ
ーズの部署」
Harvard-affiliated hospital
「ハーバード大学付属の病院」
powerhouse「大手の」

The internet giant said Monday that its Amazon Web Services unit is working with a Harvard-affiliated hospital in 5 Boston to test how AI can simplify medical care. It is the latest sign of powerhouse tech companies like Amazon and Google deepening their reach into America's $3.5 trillion healthcare market.

While the tech industry has high hopes that powerful 10 computing tools can improve diagnoses and treatment, Beth Israel Deaconess Medical Center's first projects with Amazon are less about sophisticated therapies and more about making day-to-day tasks like patient scheduling more cost-effective. 15

senior leader「上級幹部」

"We're identifying the right problems where machine learning truly can help," said Taha Kass-Hout, senior leader for healthcare and AI at Amazon.

grant「補助金」

The Seattle-based tech behemoth gave the medical center a grant valued at as much as $2 million to experiment with 20 machine learning and AI.

underutilized「活用されてい
ない」
attorney「弁護士」
Baker Donelson「ベーカー・
ドネルソン法律事務所」

"We are going to see more and more of the tech companies trying to explore different ways to partner with healthcare because there are so many untapped and underutilized markets in which they can grow," said Alisa Chestler, an 25 attorney at Baker Donelson who focuses on healthcare and technology.

appointment「予約」
in-demand specialist「売れ
っ子の専門医」

Amazon's tools are now helping Beth Israel Deaconess book operating room time more precisely and predict when patients are likely to miss appointments with its most in- 30 demand specialists. The software can also help find needed paperwork like patient-consent forms in a stack of scanned documents before surgery and alert staff if they are missing or incomplete.

patient-consent form 「患者
の同意書」

The approach has already helped the medical center expand the capacity of its 41 operating rooms, said John 5 Halamka, executive director of the Health Technology Center at Beth Israel Lahey Health.

a stack of... 「多量の〜」

executive director 「専務理
事」

For example, patients who need appendectomies are typically scheduled for an hour in surgery. But young, otherwise healthy people often need less time. "If I look at a 10 million patients, and discover we only need 25 minutes, wouldn't that be better for society? Because now the OR is the most expensive place in a hospital," Halamka said.

Bloomberg

● Summary

以下の空所 1 〜 4 に当てはまる語を選択肢から選び、書き入れましょう。

Hospitals in the United States are partnering with (1.   ) tech firms to investigate if and how (2.   ) intelligence can make a positive contribution to the day-to-day running of the hospital. The healthcare industry represents a lucrative (3.   ) market for the tech companies, which have achieved some success in making scheduling and data retrieval more (4.   ).

| efficient | untapped | artificial | huge |

以下の1〜3の英文の（　　）内に当てはまる人物名を選択肢から選び、書き入れましょう。

1. (   ) said that Amazon's AI tools have already helped Beth Israel Deaconess achieve increased efficiency in hospital operating room use.

2. (   ) expects more tech companies to look for new business partners in the field of healthcare.

3. (   ) is in charge of exploring ways to deepen collaboration between technology and healthcare at Amazon.

Taha Kass-Hout   Alisa Chestler   John Halamka

本文の内容に合うように、1と3の英文を完成させるのに適当なものを、2の質問の答えとして適当なものをa〜dから選びましょう。

1. Amazon's partnership with the hospital has so far involved
    a. providing virtual diagnosis training for junior doctors.
    b. collaborating with Google to deepen the hospital's reach.
    c. applying its expertise to the logistics of running a hospital.
    d. using AI to identify potentially useful therapies.

2. Which of the following is NOT a problem mentioned in the article?
    a. Scheduled appointments being missed
    b. Incomplete paperwork
    c. Not being able to locate documents before surgery
    d. Operating rooms being double-booked

3. The data gathered has been used to
    a. support a proposal to build an additional 41 operating rooms.
    b. reduce instances of healthy people receiving unnecessary surgery.
    c. indicate cases in which allocated time in the OP could be shorter.
    d. decrease the number of appendectomies by one million.

Acknowledgements

All the news materials are reprinted by permission of

The Ahahi Shimbun, Kyodo News, The Japan News, The Japan Times, The Associated Press, AFP-JIJI Press, Reuters and Bloomberg.

TEXT CREDITS

Chapter 1　Books! Bringing a Bright Future to Children
Japanese teen funds library for Cambodian school out of her pocket
  The Asahi Shimbun, Novermber 13, 2018

Chapter 2　Brew Sake with Fresh Ideas!
Foreign pair bring energy and fresh ideas to the table in Japan's traditional sake industry
  Kyodo News, January 04, 2019

Chapter 3　A Unique Tour Guide
'Rock star' guide offers boat tours of fanciful formations
  The Japan News, July 15, 2018

Chapter 4　A Banana with an Edible Peel
Banana with edible skin gaining popularity
  The Asahi Shimbun, August 13, 2018

Chapter 5　Too Crowded to Carry it on our Backs!
Back to front for manners on Japanese public transport
  The Japan Times, December 12, 2018

Chapter 6　Monitoring Kid's Phone Use
Do you know what your kid's doing on their phone?
  The Associated Press, June 26, 2018

Chapter 7　Learn about your Pet Dog at the Museum
New dog museum unleashed in New York City
  The Associated Press, January 12, 2019

Chapter 8　Dream of Space Tourism Comes True
New era for space tourism: Flights from Virgin Galactic and Blue Origin could come in 2019
  AFP-JIJI, July 13, 2018

Chapter 9　Save the World from Garbage!
Japanese firms see opportunity in S.E. Asia garbage
  The Japan News, January 28, 2019

Chapter 10　Manga Featuring the Elderly
Manga starting to feature elderly characters
  Kyodo News, July 17, 2018

本書には音声CD（別売）があります

Insights 2020
世界を読むメディア英語入門2020

2020年1月20日 初版第1刷発行
2020年2月20日 初版第2刷発行

編著者　　村　尾　純　子
　　　　　深　山　晶　子
　　　　　椋　平　　　淳
　　　　　辻　本　智　子
　　　　　Ashley Moore

発行者　　福　岡　正　人
発行所　　株式会社　**金　星　堂**
〒101-0051 東京都千代田区神田神保町3-21
Tel. (03) 3263-3828（営業部）
(03) 3263-3997（編集部）
Fax (03) 3263-0716
http://www.kinsei-do.co.jp

編集担当　蔦原美智　　　　　　　　Printed in Japan
印刷所・製本所／萩原印刷株式会社

ISBN978-4-7647-4098-3　C1082